RED JOURNEYS
Inside the Thai Red-Shirt Movement

Claudio Sopranzetti

T0326678

SILKWORM BOOKS

ISBN: 978-616-215-035-7

Published in 2012 by
Silkworm Books
6 Sukkasem Road, T. Suthep
Chiang Mai 50200 Thailand

info@silkwormbooks.com
http://www.silkwormbooks.com

Photographs courtesy of *The Nation*

Typeset in Candara 9.5 pt. by Silk Type

Printed and bound in China

5 4 3 2 1

To my family, the given and the chosen

CONTENTS

ACKNOWLEDGMENTS

Many people made this book possible, people who share with me all the good of this book and none of the bad. First of all, the thousands of red-shirt protesters who dedicated their time to talk to me amidst the tension of a protest, to shelter me during dangerous moments, and to welcome me into their tents and homes, in and outside Bangkok. My thanks to Hoong, Pai, Adun, Mee, Glai, Por, Leek, Nit, Luum, Boon, and the many other unnamed red shirts who were my guides and protectors during those months. My utmost gratitude goes to my friends Wittawat Tucharungrot, Agnes Dherbeys, Apiwat Seangpatthasima, Daniel Feary, Sun Thapphawut, Stefano di Gregorio, Edoardo Fanti, Margherita Colarullo, Todd Ruiz, Tracy Vanity, Alice Dubot, and Dane Wetschler who often accompanied me to protest sites and shared their ideas and observations. The research behind this book has been possible thanks to the generous support of the Wenner Gren Foundation Dissertation Fellowship, the Social Science Research Council IDRF, and the Harvard Kennedy Traveling Fellowship. A number of Thai and foreign scholars and journalists constantly offered me correctives, ideas, and support. In particular, Michael Herzfeld, Pitch Pongsawat, Yukti Mukdawijitra, Viengrat Nethipo, Nick Nostitz, Felicity Aulino, Kevin Moore, Seth Mydans, Mariko Takayasu, Chris Baker, Pasuk Phongpaichit, Danny Unger, Ben Tausig, Tyrell Haberkorn, Charles Keyes, and the editors of the *New Mandala* website, Nicholas Farrelly and Andrew Walker, who offered the first board for my postings. Special thanks go to Arun Senkuttuvan, Emily Carryer, Susan Offner, and the staff of Silkworm Books who edited and tied up the messy scribbles on my blog; to Orawan Chanovit at *The Nation* for granting me permission to reproduce their front-pages, to Francesco Gregori who helped with the pictures, and Carla Betancourt who took care of the maps. Finally, the biggest debt of gratitude goes to my family and my girlfriend, who have supported me, often waiting with bated breath for my calls to reassure them that I was fine. To them I dedicate this book.

PREFACE

I arrived in Thailand for the first time in 2004, one of the many backpackers who pass through the country every year, often looking for nothing more than a place far away from home. Unlike most backpackers, I had previously read quite a bit about Thailand, started learning its language, and written an undergraduate thesis on the relationship between the Buddhist Sangha and political structures in Siam. I was planning to spend two months traveling the country and learning Thai, but I often got stuck among Western kids who kept talking about Thailand, without practically ever having spoken to a Thai, besides guesthouse staff and occasional vendors. I kept quiet and let my frustrations grow.

As soon as my Thai started to take its first clumsy steps, a new world opened to me. Pages and pages of books I had read, complex theories, and long-overheard discussions seemed to take life, or at times lose it, when confronted with real situations, people's struggles, and daily events. Suddenly the beaches, the parties, and the backpackers' tours lost their attraction. I changed my flight and found a small room in a house of Thai students and activists in Bangkok, away from the tourist areas but close enough to speak English and find good bread when occasionally cultural differences made the cohabitation hard. Chance and vague interests had catapulted me into the midst of a civil society political group, at that time mostly voicing criticism of Prime Minister Thaksin Shinawatra. I remained in Thailand for six months. From a small room in Bangkok I prepared for my admission exams for PhD programs in anthropology, and started exploring the city and its criss-crossing of people, goods, ideas, and lifestyles. To this city and this country I have dedicated the last seven years of my life, making it my second home and an object of study. I have struggled, and still struggle, to make sense of the ongoing political transformation, one day at a time. I came to realize that the more I knew the less I understood, and that every question and doubt brought me to other questions, rarely providing answers but leaving me with a need to describe and narrate what I saw and experienced.

In September 2009, after years of summer visits, I moved to Thailand in order to conduct my ethnographic fieldwork on the lives of motorcycle-taxi drivers in the city and the various villages that most of them come from. Following the drivers' navigation of Bangkok's urban landscape as well as the rural landscape of northeastern Thailand, my research inevitably crossed the red-shirt mobilizations over and over again. At first I started going to rallies following some of my driver friends, slowly getting acquainted with the rhythms of the protests, their rhetoric, and characters. Later, as I realized the political and social potential of the movement, especially outside Bangkok, I started following the new social movement more closely, spending hours and hours at occasional protests and meetings. In March 2010, when the "One Million March" converged on Bangkok's streets from villages, towns, and urban neighborhoods, revealing the red-shirts as the biggest Thai social movement to date, this side interest took my thesis hostage and became part of my daily routine, syncopated by visits to the protest and redaction of long notes on the unfolding events. At the beginning of April, as the protest now controlling the whole of Ratchadamnoen Avenue turned violent, I realized that those notes were more than just my reflections and needed to be diffused as historical documents, narrating a human side of the red shirts' movement which often remains obscured. Suddenly the eyes of the world were focused on Thailand, but almost no one seemed to be narrating the details that my notes contained.

Mainstream Thai history often sees reality and its transformations as orchestrated by only a few "big people." In particular, political movements often end up being described and analyzed through their leaders and ideologies, successes and pitfalls, resounding actions and bombastic declarations. What is often left out are the people, the unique and yet united human beings who make up "the crowd," give it its strengths, its weaknesses, and also its flavors, smells, colors, and voices. Squeezed in between the journalistic search for the scoop and what sells, the social scientists' quest for a coherent and explanatory narration of the past and the ever-growing pornography of violence broadcast worldwide, the protesters' fears, hopes, dreams, courage, silliness, and quests for meaning often get lost in the folds of history, perennially erased from collective memory.

With this in mind I decided to establish a blog called *The Drop*, offering long descriptions of life in and around the red shirts' protests during the months of April and May 2010, as seen and understood through the eyes of a young PhD student who, as a *farang* (foreigner), dedicated years of his life to meet, listen, and try to understand Thailand and its people. It was made of occasional encounters, stolen conversations hidden in small parks with sounds of the Thai army's rifles in the background, long evenings at protest sites, slow hot afternoons on melting asphalt, or night walks among Thai soldiers—small events that history seldom archives and journalists often find too mundane to report. The book you hold in your hands is a collection of those entries and other texts previously unpublished.

To my surprise, the blog attracted thousands of readers and soon people started writing to urge me to continue. For a month and a half between April 10, and May 21, 2010, the blog became my work. Every day I would leave the house early in the morning and ride my bike across the city, scribble notes and then come back home and edit them before posting on my blog during the night. Day after day as the protest escalated, I felt a need to keep posting on current events, both to record them and to keep me sane. Every night the tension, fear, frustration, and anger accumulated during the day would disperse through my fingers as they typed on the computer. Looking back on it I now realize that I was, unconsciously, already writing the book. This book stems from a need to narrate and a sense of urgency that I felt when spending time and conversing with people in the street during the three-month-long red shirts' takeover of two main physical and symbolic spaces in Bangkok: Ratchadamnoen Avenue, the long boulevard that is traditionally a theater of big political protests for the city and the country; and the Ratchaprasong area, the high-end commercial core of the city that was for the first time transformed into a political arena. Reading newspapers and talking with academics and journalists made me realize the utmost importance of narrating every human aspect of the city experiencing the red-shirt movement that I could record, store, and describe. Far from either celebrating or dismissing the red-shirt movement, this book is an attempt, by definition incomplete, to mediate between the powerful and meaningful experiences of some of those people involved in the protest and the feebleness of their memories when the bulldozer of history starts rolling.

INSIGHTFUL, IN TREND, INDEPENDENT

THE NATION

THAILAND FRIDAY, May 21, 2010 / 32 PAGES, 1 SECTION, VOLUME 35, NO 52604 / B130

TIME TO REBUILD

Curfew extended until tomorrow, from 9pm to 5am

» **Veera and Weng** among the red-shirt leaders to surrender

Amid discord, let us together rediscover note of harmony

THE NATION

COMMENT

I t is the morning of May 20, 2010, the day after the Royal Thai Army dispersed the red shirts from the Ratchaprasong area, leaving behind fifty-five dead bodies. In the surreally-empty area, military trucks fill the air with their baritone roaring. Small pieces of paper fly everywhere, often landing in big water puddles that reflect the Central World complex, still burning. A pungent smell of burned plastic and stagnant water permeates the intersection, giving unmistakable concreteness to what looks like an apocalyptic movie. A few cleaners roam around among journalists and curious people.

The stage sits in the middle of the intersection like a skeleton. In front, plastic chairs remain scattered, facing different directions like a small crowd of confused human beings. Plastic mats roll along the ground and a huge black plastic sheet protecting the stage from the sun and snipers swings with the breeze. A massive banner in English, red with white letters, hangs over the scene, half detached from the skywalk. It declares: PEACEFUL PROTESTERS, NOT TERRORISTS.

Chairs, tents, shacks, banners, half-eaten bowls of rice, mats, clappers, fans, screens, TVs, radios, and clothes litter the intersection as during the protest. What is missing are the red-shirt protesters. Vanished.

Walking down Rama I Road in the direction of Siam Square, I pass small groups of soldiers, young guys with scared and confused looks on their faces, sweating in their camouflage fatigues. In the middle of the street is a carton filled with small bottles of Red Bull, transformed into mini-Molotovs, and capped with a few wooden slings and metal bars, ready to be photographed. Across the street is Wat Pathum Wanaram. This temple, surrounded by skyscrapers and shopping malls, was designated by the government as a "safe area" for red shirts who wanted to retreat, but yesterday it became a theater of six deaths in one of the most unclear circumstances of the whole protest. Today it is home only to abandoned objects and empty except for a group of anti-riot police relaxing in the shade. On the other side of the street, the police headquarters shelters the last groups of red-shirt protesters still in the area. The large open space outside the police headquarters is packed with people sitting everywhere, clinging to small plastic bags filled with what they could recoup in the final rush. They wait, confused, hoping to be sent back to their homes. The process has already taken some hours and most of the protesters from other regions have already been moved. I sit with a small group, close to the entrance. Two old women pass bottled water, in silence. Their faces do not smile. They stare around with wet eyes. A man sits on their left, on a portable chair. He lives in Din Daeng District, a few kilometers away from here, yet unreachable during recent days. He hasn't had a chance to go home in a week, it's too dangerous to go in that direction since the military surrounded the area.

"Why are you still here?" I ask, puzzled. "Police tell us to stay here. Things are not yet safe." He points his eyes to the gate I just came through, a few meters away. "Before, we didn't believe the police but now we believe them. This morning a police officer told us not to go out and grab our stuff, to remain in the area and not trust anyone. Two men did not trust the police and believed they could go home. They went out and were shot dead in Ratchaprasong. So now we stay here until they tell us to go."

His dark eyes, squared into thin metallic glasses, move restlessly underneath untidy gray hair. "Yesterday we stayed at the temple." He speaks softly. "We stayed close to the monks, thinking it was the safest place, but the military have no problem. The soldiers shoot monks too. In Din Daeng also they were shooting at monks." He stops. "Where is fairness? We are a peaceful group. We have no weapons. Look around you. Yet the army shoots at us." I sit down close to him. His wife passes around biscuits to me and a Thai friend of mine. "Only dictators kill like this. Snipers against people with bare hands. There is no fairness. Look at the dead. When a yellow shirt died they gave a national funeral and money to the family. If we die nobody cares." "How do you feel now?" I ask. "Look around you. Look at people's faces," he says. I look around.

Lost faces wrinkle into a short smile when they notice I am staring at them and then go back to their tense expression. "We will not accept this," he adds. "We will fight again." I stand up and say goodbye, wishing him good luck. My middle-class Thai friend, surprised by the role of the police and the complete trust given to them by the protesters, walks to a police officer standing in a white shirt at the entrance of a small building. "The people really trust the police," he says to the officer. The policeman laughs as he directs a woman with a small baby in her hands to a bathroom inside the building.

We walk around and notice that the silent groups are patrolled by border police. Two young officers in dark green uniforms are checking everybody's documents before directing them to the right buses to go home. They are from Tak Province, near the Burmese border. "We came here about a week ago," they say. "The other night we had to hide like everybody else behind the wall of the headquarters. There is nothing we can do. We have no weapons." If you close your eyes for a second you would believe you are hearing red-shirt protesters talk.

We move to the side of a building that opens onto Henry Dunant Road. Loudspeakers declare that people from Bangkok are now free to go home. Nobody seems to be in a rush to leave. The small open space is full of people sitting, standing, squatting, waiting to finally get out of this place, yet too scared to walk away. A woman's voice shouts: "People from Udon, your bus is ready." A small crowd moves towards the gate, almost unwillingly. A disorganized line of border police officers, mostly women, check everybody's ID and write down their name and province, before letting them out of the gate. The government uses female officers when the situation needs to be handled calmly, as a deterrent against conflict. It was a woman's voice, speaking from a helicopter flying over the protest area, that yesterday advised the protesters to go back home and accept defeat. Right outside the gate of the police headquarters a big pickup distributes water bottles to the protesters. Few of them take a bottle, worried that it may get them sick, as they later explain to me. Fear and paranoia often dress alike.

It is a small exodus. Composed and silent lines of people, carrying whatever they could grab before they were dispersed, walk down the empty streets with big plastic bags on their backs. The Udon group stands on the sidewalk waiting for their bus. An old man leads the group, carrying a pack of water bottles under his arm—not the ones just distributed—and a big gray bag. "We won't accept this," he says out loud. "We will continue to fight. Maybe not here in Bangkok. We will break into small groups all around the country. It is far from the end." His light blue shirt features a cat in a graduation gown with the words, "Congratulations. You have proven that you can make it with nothing more than… " The group gets on an old public bus going to the train station, on their way back home after about three months spent sleeping, eating, cheering, listening, and running for their lives on the streets of a giant and unwelcoming city. The twelve-hour trip ahead of them will be a time to reflect, to process what has happened in these last days, or just to sit in silence. I need to be there. I go back home, grab a small bag, and drive to the train station.

I arrive at Hualamphong train station at about 4:00 p.m. The spacious hall is full of people, with a tight crowd sitting on the ground in the middle of the station underneath a huge painting of King Rama V. I ask around as to whether the trains with the protesters have already departed. Most of them have left, but the train to Udon is leaving at about 8.25 p.m. I walk back to the people sitting on the ground and ask who is going to Udon. Pretty soon I am seated with a group of about twenty people heading for that province. They come and go, taking off their shoes before sitting as if they are still in the "We Love Udon" tent that hosted them for the last two months, near Lumphini Park. They all look demoralized, worn out, and unsure about what's next.

I start talking to a young man named Boon. Long hair and beautifully shaped dark eyes. He speaks quietly in a polite but firm voice. The people around him listen, occasionally throwing some sentences into the conversation. Boon is from a small village near Udon. He has been in Bangkok for more than two months, leaving a home with ten *rai* of land from which he gets enough rice to feed himself and sell, making some extra money and food by raising chickens and fish. "I wasn't here last year," he says, staring at me, "but this time it was too much. So I came to Bangkok to protest." "Had you been to Bangkok before?" "I used to live here. I worked as a security guard. Life here was too chaotic for me. I always went back home with a headache. So I decided to go back home and live in the countryside." When I ask whether he has a family or kids, he smiles. "I haven't thought about a girlfriend in a long time. It's difficult with women, you never understand each other and I want to have a calm life." "What about your parents?" Boon's eyes become opaque for a second. "They died twenty-five years ago." This makes him nine or ten years old when his parents departed. "We have been alone since then, me and my two sisters. One is married to a *farang* (foreigner) and lives in Finland now, looking after her husband's strawberry farm. He has a problem with alcohol but she has a good life. I even learned some Finnish so I can talk to my niece when she comes to visit. The other one is still in Udon. She is married so I live alone now." "Are you happy about going home?" Boon stops for a second. "We came here to bring democracy and we go back without having obtained that. Many people died. Soldiers killed them. We are all very sad." I turn around and the small crowd is listening, eyes to the ground.

An older woman takes up the conversation. "What is this? Killed casually by soldiers. We are Thai and we get killed by snipers. It is bad, very bad. The government has double standards." One after the other everybody says something about what just happened, asking for my opinion on the events and how the "people of the world" feel about Thailand. I mutter something, doubtful I can speak for the people of the world. Two men in black shirts come around. "We will fight again," they say, trying to raise the morale of the group. "It is not finished," the young man echoes. "We are going home now but no one has won or lost yet." "What next then?" "We will keep fighting against this government and the *ammat* (Thai aristocracy). Maybe not in Bangkok but we will divide into small groups all around the country and keep burning things if we need to. There is nothing else we can do. The government doesn't accept our requests and kills the people. We are unarmed, there is nothing else we can do, and now we know that peaceful protests don't work. If we are peaceful we just die." The conversation dies out and a dense silence falls over the small group as an old woman repeats with a soft voice, "We won't accept this. We cannot accept this. Red shirts cannot lose." This retreat has the bitter taste of a defeat. Days and days spent in a hostile city, overlooked by towering buildings, symbols of a life they cannot share, from which death descended upon them by the hands of snipers. A younger woman distributes food to the group and asks if everybody is ok.

Behind me a woman sits on her dirty clothes. Her feet are bare. "They are in Ratchaprasong," she says. "I ran to the temple without shoes and I was too scared to go back to get them." The young woman keeps walking around delivering small packages of rice and pork. "The people in Bangkok have helped us," a young man breaks the silence. "Many came to bring food, water, and to offer money. This time the government has seen that it is not only about Isan or Thaksin and that the population will not accept everything they do. We did not achieve democracy but we have not accepted what the government did. This will go on." The young woman comes back, distributing medicines to anyone who wants them. "You see," another woman says, "if we didn't know her we wouldn't take the food or medicine. They already tried to poison our drinks at Sarasin Road some days ago. We need to be very careful." The young woman walks back to her other three friends, all dressed in white and wearing hats. I go out to buy cigarettes.

As I return to the station, the radio rings out six o'clock and loudspeakers broadcast the national anthem. Everybody stands up, straight to the ceiling in this enormous hall. As the anthem ends one man in the red-shirt group shouts, "Ohh, Ohh, Ohh," as they did in Ratchaprasong every day after the anthem. "Ohh, Ohh, Ohh," the red shirts answer timidly. All around the atmosphere is heavy with grief, many tense faces and wet eyes in the middle of the few bags and objects that they have been able to retrieve while fleeing the advancing military tanks.

"What do you think about the leaders?" I ask. Now a big conversation erupts. Somebody says, "You need to know when to stop. The military would have killed us all, so they needed to surrender." Others say they are disappointed by leaders who run away when the military attacks. "We are not satisfied," the young man says. "We don't know what we will do next or who will be the leaders, but that is no problem, we have many leaders, in each village. I promise this is not finished." Again the situation calms down and I go out of the station with him to pick up big plastic bags full of food, delivered by a taxi driver. Boon and I distribute the last rations of food and water that people store for the long trip ahead. An older woman stands up in the middle of the crowd, and people applaud. She is eighty-two years old and she has been at the protest since March 16, sleeping on a mat on the street. "She was the oldest person in Ratchaprasong," an old woman says to me as she listens carefully to what the woman says in a barely audible voice. "We will continue to fight for democracy," she spits out of her toothless mouth, pressing her eyes to make her voice stronger, and smiles come back onto people's faces for a moment.

A well-dressed man in his forties comes around to greet people and tell them that they are not alone and that there will be other ways to fight for democracy. "He is a Phuea Thai (opposition party) MP in Khon Kaen," someone says in my ear. The man walks through the small crowd, stopping to talk to some people for a second. He *wais* (Thai traditional form of greeting) the old woman profusely, then hugs her.

It is time to board and most of those waiting walk to the four cars at the end of the train reserved for the people of the protest. "Abhisit is so generous," says a man as we step into the empty car. "He kills us first and then rewards us with special cars."

While most take their seats, a group of younger protesters remain sitting on the platform. One of them walks around displaying his bare torso covered in tattoos. This small group, both inside and outside the coach, is isolated from the world for today, connected to one another by an extreme sense of solidarity and a shared feeling of being threatened from the outside. The few bills that people still have in their pockets are collected to buy cigarettes and whiskey, indispensable for what looks like a long night. Food and drink are provided and stored in the first car. At almost every station along the route, more supplies will be delivered by someone and then distributed among the protesters. As I wait outside the train, some of the youngsters try to start a conversation in English. As soon as I tell them I can speak Thai, they launch into long political tirades against the government. They are loud, seemingly the only ones enjoying the moment. Above me many heads and hands hang out of the train windows, waiting to depart. "Enough already with Bangkok," a middle-aged woman cries out loud. Two friends, a videographer and a journalist, arrive at the station. I had called them, hoping this moment could be covered by international media, not just a young student. When one of them sets up her camera, a middle-aged guy throws himself in front of it, inebriated by the alcohol that is running—and that will run all night long—through his veins. "We are not terrorists, we are not terrorists, we are not terrorists," he shouts. "We just want democracy. Why does Abhisit kill us?" He speaks English quite well but the words come out like short mechanical single shots from a machine gun. He is overexcited, jumping around, swinging between moments of euphoria and lapses into thoughtful silence. He is wearing a worn white shirt and a black hat with a big blue towel tucked under the brim. Big amulets spill out of his shirt. He switches to Japanese and has a long conversation with my friends behind the camera. Surprises are always dressed in unexpected clothes.

From the train more people are thrusting their heads out of the window, bemused by the guy drawing big circles with his hands as he speaks. The videographer notices the onlookers and asks me to translate questions for her. She walks up to two women and tucks her camera through the window. "When did you arrive in Bangkok? How do you feel now? What do you think you will do next? How are you feeling about going home? Who is waiting for you there? What will be the first thing you do when you reach home?" With some variation, these same questions are asked of other people nearby. The two middle-aged women say they have been in Bangkok for a month and a half, staying at the protest site instead of going back and forth from home. They voice their dissatisfaction with the leadership that has abandoned them in the most difficult moment, and express their sorrow at leaving Bangkok with many dead bodies on the streets and the political situation unchanged. It is funny how the more peaceful protesters are now voicing their disappointment with their leaders, while the more *harco* (hardcore) elements seem less prone to criticize the leaders, understanding the necessity of their actions this time, as part of a "lose a battle, win the war" mentality. "What did you like the most about staying at the protest?" the reporter asks. "Sleeping in front of Erawan Hotel," they answer together and smile. "Fighting for democracy," the drunken man shouts. "The weather also," they say. "It wasn't too hot in Bangkok," maybe thinking about the hot, dry temperatures on the Isan plateau at this time of the year. "Who was the best person you met?" "We love Thaksin," they answer coyly. "But he wasn't there," I add. They laugh. "Yes, it was good to meet people from all around the country who are fighting for democracy." "What will you do now?" "We will go back, rest a little, and then keep going with our fight. We still don't know where or how. Maybe we will need new leaders but there are already younger leaders." We thank them and get on the train, where people have reserved two benches for us.

The long rows of hard seats are half-filled with people, mostly sitting, eating something, and preparing for the night. It is already 10:00 p.m. Right before departure the MP from Khon Kaen gets on board and walks through the cars, followed by three guards. He greets everyone and wishes them good luck. "It is not finished," he reassures them as he rapidly passes through. My journalist friend asks me to get his card so I go to find him in the next car. "What do you think will happen next?" "It is really hard to say. People are angry. It is hard to know what they will do." He speaks in flawless English. "But I can reassure you that these people are not defeated." He walks away. I get back to our coach as the protesters are supplying us with water bottles and food. A man who was sitting close to the young man I talked to at the train station tells me to be careful with water. "Always turn the bottle upside down and see if it drips. If it does, don't drink it—it may be poisoned." He tells me to be mindful of an incident at Sarasin Road a week ago, when during the first night of violence bottles of poisoned coffee drinks sent some protesters to the hospital. Sadness and dissatisfaction mixes with fear and paranoia on this train. People cannot trust a government that in the last two days first offered them a safe haven inside a temple and then attacked it, leaving people dead. On some occasions extreme paranoia is what keeps you alive. This feeling will accompany us for the whole trip, with rumors of possible attacks and army blocks spreading in waves inside the four cars.

Beside us the old woman I met earlier sits with the two women we interviewed. The videographer almost cries when she sees her, touched by the coincidence of finding her again after they had met in the temple, before the craziness of the last days. We have a short interview with her. She scarcely moves her toothless mouth and the words are amplified to us by two women and another man who sit close to me. "I'm a fighter," she says, "and we will fight again for democracy." The train is now starting to move into the darkness of the city, emptied by the curfew.

As the train leaves the station Boon tells me to close the windows until we get out of Bangkok and to be careful about what is outside. "Somebody could throw stones or worse," he says, staring into my eyes. "When we have left Bangkok you can pull the window down." Many times in the next few days in the provinces, Bangkok will be described to me as a dangerous place, the capital that pretends to know what is best for the whole nation, a city of privileges created by the hard work of Isan people without any gratitude, or just a place where life is tough, everything is business, and people do not care about each other. The body of this macrocephalic nation is now kicking, asking for some form of self-determination and recognition. Seen from Isan, this conflict, often described as a class struggle, seems more about regional disparities and social inequalities that are economic, legal, and educational. Many of the protesters whom I met in Ratchaprasong in the previous days, and whom I will visit while in Udon, are petty shopowners, tourist guides, small business people, and farmers with relatively productive land and concrete houses. Those struggling in the streets of Bangkok came from a growing regional lower middle class that mixes with the urban poor, sharing their demands for social equality. Their requests, even if voiced under the word "democracy," when broken down and unpacked, revolve around what we would call a "social equality" agenda, much larger than a quest for a new political structure. As one man in the train put it in a long and fascinating interview: "What we mean by democracy is fairness (*khwam yutthitham*). We want fairness in three ways: legal, political, and educational."

We pass through Bangkok without incident and so take a walk through the train, leaving our stuff in the safe hands of our friends from Udon. The videographer meets another woman she has met before. Her name is Pai, the lady without shoes I had seen at the station. She wears an oversized blue shirt and long worn out jeans. They greet each other. Pai looks as if her head is a bit slow and dazed but her heart is overflowing with emotion. She immediately starts talking of the night before at the temple, of the fear, the darkness, the shooting and explosions all around, the dead bodies. "I cried so much that I have no tears left." Her deep eyes stare at mine, completely dry. The journalist prompts me to ask if she has ever taken the Skytrain. "Why a question about the Skytrain now?" I think. I do my role as a translator and go ahead. The answer is fascinating and condenses all the perceptions of Bangkok as a dangerous foreign space. "I have never taken the Skytrain and I have never gone up to take a look at it. It means nothing to me. It is just something built to make the life of rich people easier, as if it was not already easy." A space of inequality, transformed into a source of death. This theme will run through many conversations on the train.

As we walk back to our seats an old man stops us. His T-shirt is draped across his shoulders. "See you again next year," he says in English. Back to Thai. "This is not finished yet, it is not even half done. We will come back over and over again. We are not satisfied and we cannot lose." He looks up with a confrontational face. "Red shirts cannot lose." "How are you feeling now?" "Normal," he answers with an angry face. "It is like last year. I was here then on a train going back but we will come again. The fight doesn't stop here." We walk back to our seats. A drunken policeman walks past us shouting, "We just get killed, this is what we get. Let's go home now." He stops. Tears in his eyes. "Look, I'm crying!" he shouts before covering our camera with his hand. Soon after, he is back asking to see our tickets and IDs. A man from the Udon group comes around. "Don't worry," he says, "I will look after you along the trip. I have already accepted dying, so I can very well die to protect you." He walks away, arm around the officer's shoulders. The train ride proceeds smoothly but slowly. Boon asks me to walk with him. "There is news that there may be some attack on the train. Newin's people will be waiting for us, maybe shooting at the train." Again the red shirts' worst nightmare. Newin Chidchob is a politician who allowed the present government to come to power, without popular elections, by changing sides in parliament and offering his party's support to the now governing Democrat Party. Boon reassures me that people will be vigilant. The tension is palpable, at least among the young guys who sit in between cars looking out for strange movements. Guards are thought to be needed at every step. "Where does the news come from?" I ask. "There are military on this train, red shirts dressed as civilians, and they have told us. We have to be careful until we reach Khorat. After that we are home." Khorat, the popular name for Nakhon Ratchasima, is a major city of northeastern Thailand and often nicknamed the Gateway of Isan. For them, it is also the gateway into a safe zone.

Nothing happens and slowly people fall asleep in our car. The next car, mostly filled with younger people and more hardcore reds, is sleepless. "I can't sleep," an older man tells me, "just too many images in my head." The sleepless night is helped by whiskey that flows, changing the smell of people's breath. I remain there for a while then walk up and down the train, chatting to people awake and sipping booze. A man in his sixties pulls out of his pockets some pictures from the time he was a soldier. Memories of a group of youths, weapons in their hands, the background of a forest. "I am a black shirt, and I was a mercenary before," he says, staring at me. "I used to work for the army during the communist period. After that I made a living as a guard." Silence descends. A long history of insurgency and counter-insurgency condenses in front of my eyes, embodied in this old man. I go back to my seat and fall asleep, cradled by the train.

PM REASSURES KINGDOM

» **Abhisit** vows rehabilitation, says situation improving

» **Premier** cancels Russia trip to lead restoration of peace

» **Red shirts** return home but promise to carry on struggle

A PHOTO of detained red-shirt leader Natthawut Saikua, circulated in social media such as Facebook, Pantip and OKNation blogging site, shows him apparently enjoying himself at a police guest house in Phetchaburi.

THE POLICE guest house in Phetchaburi's Nonnuwat Cana where red leaders are being detained.

Uproar as red-shirt leaders have an easy life

ON PAGE 2A
» Victims to rally for govt aid
» 65 killed since rally started on March 12

ON PAGE 3A
» Financial aid being planned
» Curfew exacerbates tourism woes

ON PAGE 6A
» Photos of the aftermath

I wake up with the most stunning of sunrises reflected on the wet rice fields outside Khorat. Everybody around me seems to be awake already, eating their breakfast or still sipping from a bottle. The man who can speak Japanese stands in front of the window and shouts in English, "We are in the free zone!" I grab my camera and start shooting out of the window.

"This is not very beautiful," a man tells me, "you can't even see the sun coming up." It looks gorgeous to me. The moment is magic as the light enters the car and is absorbed by the dark orange robes of two monks. "We are in the red zone," the journalist says, staring at the red sky out of the window. Others do the same. Faces finally relax as their noses fill with the fresh smell of the countryside. More food is served.

My friends propose another round of interviews. A man sits close to us as we start asking him questions. We have a very long talk in which he lays out the foundations of the red shirts' movement, from the 2006 military coup that removed their beloved prime minister, Thaksin; to the new military constitution in 2007; the next election won by Thaksin's side under the new name, the People's Power Party; and the judiciary's intervention into politics resulting in the dismantling of the party. He goes on to describe the yellow shirts' protest against this elected government; the parliamentary reshuffling that brought the current prime minister, Abhisit, to power without elections; the expansion of the red-shirt movement, and all the way to the present. His story is laced with criticisms of the double standards in this country and the lack of fairness in the system. He speaks softly, no anger in his voice, just a very sober analysis of the history of the relationship between poor and rich in this country and the demands of the people who feel excluded from the system. Education recurs as the main cause of inequality.

"But life in Isan is better than it used to be twenty or thirty years ago, right? You have television, electricity?" we ask. "Yes we have a better life, we are richer, and we have things we didn't have in the past." "So life is easier now?" "It is not, life is more difficult now. When I was a kid life was easy. You just grew rice, caught fish, and you could live there. Now is different. You need to send your kids to school, save for chemicals to put in the field, have money for petrol. The whole world has developed, and so has Isan, but we are slower than Bangkok so we remain behind." "So what has changed now?" "In the past, five or six years ago, things were better, we could get money and the government had policies for us. Now this government is not interested in us." He keeps comparing the present with the time when Thaksin was in power but somehow managing never to name him.

"Did you get around while you were in Bangkok?" "No," he answers. "I stayed only in Ratchaprasong, walking up and down the protest area." "Did you like the Ratchaprasong area?" "No. The buildings there are too tall. You couldn't do anything. Snipers were there and there was nothing we could do." His answers mix urban design, taste, and protest strategies. We keep talking for a while until he says he needs to go to the bathroom and walks away, probably tired of our questions.

I start chatting with a younger guy, about sixteen years old, who sat listening through the previous interview. "I like Bangkok," he says with bright eyes as soon as the other man walks away. "You can go have fun wherever you want. There are so many people." "Would you want to go back if you have a chance?" I ask. "Yes," he says, feeling the attraction of the metropolis that millions of people around the world share with him, including me. I sit thinking about this and fall asleep again.

When I wake up the train has stopped in the middle of nowhere and some people have gotten off, waiting underneath small trees at the side of the tracks. Others are walking through the fields to reach a road where they can try to catch a ride to their villages. Others just lean out of the windows. I guess we have been there for a while. I get off with Boon. He pulls out a pair of binoculars and looks past the train to check if there is some sort of military block. We stay there for a while, burning in the hot sun. Suddenly, a crowd gathers. Two young men start fighting in front of the train. Apparently one of them has been bothering and insulting others on the train all night long, inebriated by alcohol. Now in the heat, nerves have exploded. The drunken one picks up a big rock and runs towards one of the windows. Other people get out of the train. The small scuffle goes on for a while, including some kicks and a hilarious chase in the nearby field, with many people falling on the ground, ending with the drunken guy and three of his friends reaching the street and hitching a ride. These have been a very hard couple of months for everybody and finally the tension of the last days is slowly easing.

The train starts moving backwards, gets a new locomotive, and heads again in the right direction. We are close to home. The atmosphere gets tense again as news comes in that the military are waiting at the train station in Udon. After a discussion, the protesters decide to get off at various small stations before Udon in order to leave the soldiers puzzled over the disappearance of the red shirts. Boon and the other people I sat with at Hualamphong invite me to go to the house of one older woman, rest a bit, and eat together before heading with him to the house of my motorcycle-taxi friend who lives in the countryside outside Udon, where I will sleep that night. I accept. Despite all their sorrow and sadness for what happened in the last few days and for having to leave the city without having achieved what they went there for, the happiness and relief of arriving home after months away puts smiles back on people's faces as they poke their heads out of the windows and simmer down in the winds of home. "I haven't seen my husband for two months," says the old woman who will host us, as her beautiful wrinkles curve around her mouth. We stop in a small station and get off, about ten of us. For the first time in several days the tourist slogan about a "Land of Smiles" does not sound like a bad joke.

We sit in little chairs in front of the station as the train leaves, say farewell to the others, and walk out. A small dirt road leads into the countryside. It is raining, an omen of luck and an indispensable factor in the agricultural economy. We will discover later that it had not rained for a while, making this day even more extraordinary. Outside the station four *tuk-tuk* are parked, with no drivers. We sit waiting for the husband of the old woman to pick us up. The man who speaks Japanese almost cannot stand up straight, worn out by a long night of drinking. He is nervous and keeps speaking rudely to everyone in the group. People try to ignore it, squatting on the ground and smelling the scent of rain. Boon walks to me and draws me to one side. "I don't like people who drink," he says. "They always treat people badly." We stand there in the light rain, smoking a cigarette.

I feel very fortunate to have met Boon. In his face, marked by the stress and difficulties of his life—from losing his parents when he was young to being alone now in the world on his small farm—I see the signs of a new Thailand to be: thoughtful, compassionate, yet firm in its ideals. The drunken man pushes someone, and another tries to calm him down. "We are among ourselves," they say. One of the women sits on the ground, singing a sad song in a beautiful voice.

A blue pickup pulls into the dirt road and stops in front of us. The husband gets out, an old man with gray hair and a black sleeveless shirt. He looks at his wife from behind the car door. She looks back with a smile. We get in the pickup, four people in the front and eight in the back. The youth fascinated by Bangkok sits close to me, wearing a black shirt with the face of Nattawut, one of the red-shirt leaders, pasted onto the body of a *muay thai* (Thai boxing) fighter, kicking a man with the face of Abhisit, the current prime minister. He is worried that he may have trouble wearing that shirt if we run into a military roadblock. The man who told me he would protect me on this trip takes off his white shirt and proposes an exchange. He puts on the black shirt and stands up, shouting to the small village, "Red shirts are back," with his fists in the air. Some people from the street applaud.

The husband drives carefully. We fight with the wind to light our cigarettes. A guy picks up one of the bottles of water in front of us and dials a number on an imaginary keypad. "Hello Abhisit," he says, "how are you my friend?" Everybody laughs. "I haven't seen you in a while. How are you?" He turns to me. "We studied together in England," he whispers, covering the bottle with his hand. More laughter. "Hmm... Hmmm... where are you now? Really? Why aren't you home? Ohhh... you can't go back there... The people don't accept that you kill them... hmmm...

What buffaloes!" Everybody cracks up. People inside the car open a small window to hear what is going on. "Yeah... yeah... that is very bad. I see..." He stops for a second listening to what Abhisit is saying. "I just wanted to ask you a favor. Could you please send a helicopter to pick me up? Hmmm... Hmmm.... Why can't you? Ohh... they are all busy flying over Ratchaprasong." Again people crack up as he also bursts into laughter. People clap. "You should do this on TV, maybe for People Channel," I tell him. People are clearing their tears with their thumbs and index fingers. The guy is an endless well of comic relief. As we drive along, he calls Prime Minister Abhisit, Deputy Prime Minister Suthep, Army Chief Anupong, and the head of the Privy Council Prem on water-bottle phones in both his hands. He is hilarious and my self-appointed personal guard delights the small crowd that starts laughing as soon as he picks up another bottle, before he even says a word. He stands up and shouts, "People, don't be afraid. The red shirts are back," imitating the rhetoric of the red shirts' leaders on stage. We stop at a sleepy petrol station and he gets down from the truck, dancing to the music of a small radio. Again, everybody laughs. We drive off again and stop in a small market.

As we park the car a policeman asks us for news from the red camp in Bangkok. Two of the people in the truck stand in front of a small temple in the parking lot, praying. We enter the market and buy grilled chicken, papaya salad, and two leaf-envelopes full of bugs and fat ants. "They are delicious," the woman says. "Try some." They taste quite bland but I nod, smiling. We get back in the pickup and drive home. Pai, the woman without shoes, carries a small plastic bag. "What did you buy?" I ask. "A phone charger," she answers, "but it cost 120 baht so I cannot buy shoes now." Strange priorities, I think. "She hasn't been able to call her mom," the young man says as if he is reading my mind. "She must be very worried."

We finally get home, tired by the long trip. It is a big brick house with a nice fence around it, not very far from the main street. Again, these are definitely not the poor Isan farmers that the media describes. We get off the pickup and carry our stuff inside the house. The woman's daughter comes out with a big smile to greet her mother. Dogs jump on her, unable to constrain their happiness even in the presence of strangers. We walk inside the fence and sit in a wooden *sala*, a Thai open pavilion, in front of the house. As the woman goes inside the house we freshen up with some water collected in a big jar outside the house. "It's rainwater," the young man keeps repeating to me.

We go back to the *sala* and sit waiting for food as a dense silence descends upon the group, a silence that only the countryside can offer. Everybody looks down. An older man starts talking, without raising his eyes, in a hoarse monotonous voice. "They killed so many of us. We will never know how many. They just shot at everybody they could." His eyes are glued to the mat, his voice low. "But we will not stop, we will keep fighting. We cannot lose." I have no idea if the others are listening. "I am not from here. I am from Surin but there is nothing going on there so I came here, to see what is going on and what will happen next. I am not sure how or when but we will keep fighting. We cannot lose." The silence is broken by a voice from inside the house. "Chicken. Who can help us cut it?" I stand up to help and the man speaking does not seem to notice me leaving. Soon everything is on the small mat and we start eating. The guy who speaks Japanese, back into a decent state, puts on a VCD of the violence at the protest on April 10. Not the best choice for this lunch.

Right after lunch Boon tells me we should go. I pick up my things and say goodbye to everyone, thanking them for their help over the past day. We exchange phone numbers and they ask me to let them know if something happens in Bangkok. We hop on a motorcycle that the woman offered us, driven by the youth now in the other guy's T-shirt. He drives us to the big street nearby and leaves the two of us there, waiting for a bus. We stand on the side of the street talking about our lives, our passions, our fears. I've known Boon only since yesterday but I feel very comfortable with him, and he seems to share the feeling. Once in a while he pulls the binoculars from his pocket and looks at the street, hoping to see a bus coming. "It's arriving," he says, "pick up your bag."

An old, slow blue bus stops a few meters away. As we are about to enter through the back door, the ticket woman rushes out of the front door and jumps on Boon, hugging him tightly. "I thought you were dead," she says with a broken voice. "I thought I would never see you again." She squeezes his shoulders, running her fingers through his long hair. "I went to the station three times asking for you. They told me to wait for the names of the dead to come in." He turns around to me, as her face sinks into his chest. "She is my sister," he tells me, trying to avoid tears. "He is a journalist friend." "Hey," she says, "I thought I would never see you again," hugging him tight. They stand there, embracing, looking away from each other to hide the tears that fill their eyes. I walk away a bit and sit down, leaving them to this moment, as other people sit in the crowded bus, ignoring them. After a few miles' drive, Boon says, "I live here," pointing to a small two-story concrete house at the side of the road. "Thank you so much for everything," I respond as he gets off the bus. I wave to him from the bus window as Boon sets foot on his land, at last.

Looking back

Why did this man, and many others with him, leave behind their land, houses, jobs, and families to live uncomfortably for months on the asphalt pavements of the capital? Who are the men and women who comprise the red-shirt movement? Why and how did they take to the streets in Bangkok? How did the city react to their presence? What are their motivations, hopes, dreams, angers, and demands? How did all of this end up in a bloody massacre? To answer these questions we have to go back and retrace the journeys of some red-shirt supporters who shared, fought, and clashed during the two-month-long protests in Bangkok between March and May 2010, only to leave behind the bodies of fellow protesters, journalists, army officers, and a changed political and physical landscape in Bangkok, and in the whole country.

Deciding where to start, looking for the seed that generated a tree is always a partial and questionable enterprise. This story for me began with the September 19, 2006, military coup that removed from power the prime minister with the strongest support in Thai history up to now, Thaksin Shinawatra, leader of the Thai Rak Thai Party. As he was in New York getting ready to deliver a speech at the United Nations, military tanks rolled into Bangkok without shooting a single round. Pictures of Thai and foreigners posing with soldiers traveled around the world. People looked puzzled at the bizarre scene, at odds with Thaksin's previous landslide electoral victory.

Protests in the days after the military intervention were few and scattered, mostly by radical intellectuals, activists, and students. A small protest occurred on September 20 at Democracy Monument, followed by another one at Siam Center and on the grounds of Thammasat University, where undercover army officers outnumbered the protesters. On November 1, 2006, a lonely protest against the coup took place. Praiwan Nuamthong, a taxi driver who had previously driven his car into a military tank at Royal Plaza, hanged himself under a pedestrian flyover on the Vibhavadi-Rangsit Highway, leaving a note opposing the coup. A few weeks later three anti-coup groups started to stage a series of protests around the old city, reaching a peak on December 10 (Constitution Day), when about two thousand people dressed in black gathered in Sanam Luang, the big grounds in front of the Royal Palace, to express opposition to the coup. It was not, however, until June 15, 2007, that the United Front of Democracy Against Dictatorship (UDD) was created, merging Thaksin's supporters and pro-democracy activists.

After a violent confrontation with the PAD on September 2 at the Makkhawan Bridge along Ratchadamnoen Avenue, this new group, at this point still not associated with the color red, halted its rallies before the December 2007 election. Protests revived in May 2008 to defend the right of Samak Sundaravej's elected government to stay in power despite the mounting protests at Government House by the yellow-shirted PAD. The protests continued as the political instability progressed toward the installation, in December 2008, of a new unelected government headed by Abhisit Vejjajiva, thanks to the defection of Newin Chidchob and twenty-two MPs in his faction from the majority party. The UDD, now also known as the red shirts, reacted to the new political landscape by increasingly, yet slowly, departing from direct support to Thaksin and moving toward more fundamental issues of democracy and equal opportunity.

On March 26, 2009, the red shirts set up a permanent protest camp in front of Government House, similar to the one previously established by the PAD to remove the elected government. The red shirts demanded Abhisit's resignation. On April 8, more than a hundred thousand people participated in a red-shirt rally in front of Government House and at the adjacent Royal Plaza, while parallel rallies were held in a dozen provincial centers. During the night, mobility in the city was brought to a halt by a crowd of taxi and motorcycle-taxi drivers, who took over the key transportation node of Victory Monument. Urban flows, the quintessential core of modern capitalism, were blocked by the very people who were supposed to facilitate them. On April 11, a group of red shirts broke into an ASEAN summit meeting in Pattaya, effectively putting the meeting to an end and forcing Thai and foreign state officials to flee. On April 13, ten thousand military troops were moved into Bangkok to "clean" the streets and re-establish urban flows. In the first serious clash between state forces and the red shirts, at least seventy people were injured and the army seemed to have won the confrontation. The protest at Government House dispersed and many observers thought that was the end of the UDD.

Contrary to the government's hopes, in the following months the UDD was completely reorganized by rebuilding its local branches, extending its presence in rural Thailand, and training its members. More than 450 "Red Shirts' Schools" were opened all around the country to develop and foster the UDD local chapters and popular outreach. Early in 2010 a number of protests were held in big cities in Isan drawing thousands of people, yet almost completely unreported in national and international news. On March 12, 2010, the red shirts announced a "Million Man March," and started to move toward Bangkok from regional centers. Caravans converged on Bangkok to stage the largest popular protest in Thai history to date. The central stage was erected at Phan Fa Bridge, a few hundred meters away from Democracy Monument and from the October 14,

1973, Memorial on Ratchadamnoen Avenue, the historical boulevard of political protest that connects Sanam Luang (Royal Grounds) to Royal Plaza, the location of the Royal Throne Hall and the Thai Parliament. From the central stage, caravans of red shirts drove through the city, inciting people to join them in protest, thus revealing the widespread support among working class urban dwellers and neighborhoods. The city was engulfed in an endless stream of red. Bikes, motorbikes, cars, trucks, and pickups turned the streets of Bangkok into a moving river of protesters. On April 3, 2010, after a series of symbolic protests around the city and an uneventful round of televised negotiations with the government, the red shirts decided to change strategy and move part of their supporters to the upscale commercial center of the city and quintessential space of inequality: the Ratchaprasong intersection and its adjacent areas.

A new stage was set up underneath the elevated Skytrain tracks, facing a huge plaza in front of Central World, the third biggest shopping mall in the world. In the days following, the protesters and their leaders juggled between the traditional space of politics around the Sanam Luang-Ratchadamnoen-Royal Plaza axis, and what they were claiming as a new political arena in the city, the Ratchaprasong intersection. Worried about the expansion of the red shirts across the city, the Royal Thai Army attempted to disperse the protesters from the Ratchadamnoen area on April 10, but failed. During a long day of confrontation, twenty-five people were killed, five of them military officers, one a Japanese videographer working for Reuters. Suddenly the eyes of the world were on Thailand, and everybody realized the seriousness of the situation and the resilience of both the national elite and the red-shirt movement, respectively protecting and challenging existing privileges. After the night of April 10, the whole movement took another form, realizing its strengths and its weaknesses. My narration starts from April 11, the day after the violent clash between the red shirts and the army in the area around Democracy Monument. The journey of the following chapters runs from this day to the day after the dispersal on May 19.

INSIGHTFUL, IN TREND, INDEPENDENT

THE NATION
ON SUNDAY

THAILAND, SUNDAY, April 11, 2010 / 24 PAGES, 3 SECTIONS, VOLUME 35, NO 52564 / B130

OUR DARKEST HOUR

Yesterday's bloodbath is a wake-up call to halt the slide towards anarchy

FIRST FATALITIES

PM mourns loss of life

> **I promise the government will carry out [the task] with transparency, fairly and in a way that benefits the country and the people.**
>
> PM ABHISIT VEJJAJIVA

ANALYSIS

RED-SHIRT, ARMY CLASHES LEAVE 11 DEAD, 678 INJURED

t's the day after. Yesterday the military intervened to try and disperse the red shirts from the Phan Fa Bridge area. The struggle left twenty-five cold bodies. As I walk home down the small, badly lit *soi* (lane), a very well- informed foreign journalist tells me on the phone, in a distant voice, "It was bad. It is the beginning of war. Their brains were splattered on the road."

"There was a brain left on the street," a young woman with small dark brown eyes, almost lost in the sea of red that colors her head, body, and neck, tells me. She is squatting, arranging a large piece of cloth covered with books on a side of Central World in the Ratchaprasong area. The books are about people's movements, an odd mixture of contemporary radical history presented in the omnipresent radical academic magazine, *Fa Diao Kan* (Same Sky), classics of Thai radicalism, old books with yellowish pages and the basics of Marxist thought, from Marx himself to Rosa Luxemburg. "They are not men. They are animals," she adds, using the most intense of Thai insults. The book vendor, an old man with large roundish glasses and worn teeth that show their metal fillings, transforming his smile into a mix of glittering silver, yellowish calcium, and black spots that reveal his life-long dependency on tobacco, stands close to her, talking to passersby. I have met him many other times at red-shirt protests, always with his selection of books to sell and a few he would not sell but which you can order as a photocopy, to be picked up at the next protest. He immediately recognizes me and, as often with foreigners, his *wai* is shortly followed by a handshake. As always, at this protest he does not only sell books but stages political debates, mostly personal tirades. He seems to enjoy my presence. The foreigner who speaks Thai offers him too good an opportunity to say how things are and slowly enlarges the discussion to include passersby who stop, listen a while, maybe buy something, and then walk away. I offer him a stable public that allows him to keep going. I think he knows that at some points I can't follow him totally, but he doesn't care. In the end, the discussion is not for me. He tells me, "This is class war, pure and simple," and the problem is not Abhisit but the people above him.

The Ratchaprasong intersection is a red sea. The stage is at the center of the intersection, and a large crowd stands around it, on the side of Pratunam market, creating a disorienting stillness in a space where mobility and rapid traffic are the norms. On top of the stage a large banner says in English: "Welcome to Thailand. We just want democracy." A message very similar to the one that the opposing yellow shirts handed to tourists during the occupation of the Bangkok International Airport in November 2008. Underneath, a larger square banner shows a fighter with open hands, in a typical Zapatista representation in stencil. A white inscription, "Peasants" (translation of *phrai*, the Thai word for commoners), stands out in the sunset from the shirt of the speaker. On the higher ground in front of Central World the crowd is thinner. People sit on the ground and listen with a less physical participation, surrounded by spaces of commerce and consumption transformed into a truly social space, a new political arena in the city, away from the traditional politics played in the old town. I walk around for a while, enjoying the feeling of this reclaimed space and chatting with people here and there. The atmosphere is calm and joyful, food being cooked, the light dimming, and the usual clapping. The first break is for the national anthem. The book vendor stands up and straightens his body but keeps talking, as many others around him do. The second break is in memory of the "heroes" who died yesterday, a long minute of complete silence. Bodies composed as for the anthem but this time not a word in the air. At the same time a funeral is going on a few kilometers away at Phan Fa Bridge, where the people were killed last night. The silence ends with a clap and everybody goes back to their activities.

People all around speak about yesterday, the attack, the violence, the dead, but as if it happened in another space or time. It hardly feels like something that took place less than twenty-four hours ago or that could still be going on where we are standing now. In one corner of the huge area, composed of the plaza in front of the Central World shopping complex and what used to be the street, there are boards with pictures from yesterday, people shot, rifles in the grip of soldiers, dead bodies wrapped in Thai flags, an empty street with a brain on the pavement, there, alone. As if it were surgically taken out of the skull and then purposefully stretched on the street so as to extend to its maximum, to cover more ground. People crowd in front of these pictures. A woman comes over to me and starts recounting what happened yesterday in English. It is the usual "we were bare-handed and they had weapons" story that people are repeating around the city. I walk away, buy some grilled pork, and hop on a motorcycle-taxi in the direction of my home. The driver is a young woman, not very used to the bike. She rides along the empty Ratchadamri Road with a basic lack of equilibrium, wearing a vest from Pathumwan District, the area around Ratchaprasong. I ask her where she works normally and she tells me that she doesn't have a fixed place. She gets the vest from a friend and does this as a side job, besides her office employment. I ask her whether she comes for the work or for the red shirts. To work, she tells me, laughing. She says there is no problem working in the protest area, "not as in the *soi*." I ask her to drop me off at the entrance of my alley, telling her that I will probably see her tomorrow.

The number of motorcycle-taxis at the protest has increased dramatically after the clash. Many of them wear a red scarf over the vest to show their multiple roles and flexible presence at the protest. In the streets around Ratchaprasong they are the only transporters because the buses and Skytrain have stopped. Many of them, however, also sit in the crowd, participating in the life of the protest. In the empty roads they move slowly, often bending backwards as the passenger bends forwards, to talk. The usually silent interaction during a ride has become something different now. It is part of the protest, part of the political participation, discussing with motorcycle-taxi riders, sources of information, travelers, and carriers. For the next month they will be the only way to move in and out of the protest, the only ones able to navigate through the endless sea of red shirts.

APRIL 12
Unlikely Allies

sit down on a side of the October 14, 1973, Memorial on Ratchadamnoen Avenue, a monument built to commemorate the massacre perpetrated by the military against students and workers who opposed the military dictatorship of General Thanom Kittikachorn. Above the monument a red banner with white script says, "October 14 initiated Democracy." The whole area between Phan Fa Bridge, where the big stage has been erected, and Sanam Luang, the spacious ground in front of the Royal Palace, is filled with protesters. Stalls, vendors, and tents of many groups who have come from the provinces to support the red shirts, fill the street. The large avenue looks like an extended village fair with music, activities, and people lounging everywhere. One major difference: in the middle of the avenue, military tanks sit in the sun. In the calm of the early afternoon an old woman walks into the small amphitheater at the center of the memorial. She is dressed in a wide purple tunic and a white veil with blue edges. From the fringes of the dress emerges dark skin with the deep wrinkles that the sun gifts to people who live close to the sea. She walks to the center of the small stage, surrounded with brown flowerpots on the gray marble pavement. She unfurls a mat, looks at the people sitting on the higher ground, eating snacks or just sitting in silence to find some peace in the middle of the crowd. Beside her a young man walks through the photos at the monument, staring at students of his age, in white button-down shirts, filling the Royal Avenue.

The woman lays her mat on the ground, facing west, the direction of Mecca, and by chance also of the Royal Palace, a few kilometers away. An older man arrives from that direction, walking away from a food stall. He stands close to her and silently takes off his white shirt, leaving his skin to glitter in the afternoon sun. There's no difference between the color of the skin on his body and on his face, a sign of his outdoor work. He quietly puts a piece of plastic on the ground, the same as people use here to sit at protest, made up of uncut food labels, and over it a red scarf. Out of a plastic bag that the woman carried he pulls a red T-shirt with the face of Thaksin stamped stencil-style in white. The face is sad. The man puts the shirt on and stands, eyes into the infinite, before starting to pray, up and down on his knees in this small oasis of silence. The old woman then takes his place and silently makes her prayers. He sits on the steps beside her, busily shuffling a rosary through his fingers. His eyes are wet. Having finished the rosary he sits there for a moment, nervously rubbing his hands, then stands up and walks away, nodding at me as he passes by. I lose track of him in the crowd. The woman gets up, holding her sarong, and quietly starts gathering their stuff. First a *Thai Rath* newspaper, then the mat, carefully folded by expert hands. She stands up, checks the bottom of her vest, picks up a bottle of water left there, and walks away in the same direction as the old man, again smiling at me as she passes by. The small round stage remains empty for a second before a small chubby kid steps in, looking for small fishes inside the lotus pots. Conflict creates strange allies. Thaksin and the red shirts are masters at this, condensing odd allies under the same flag, building their current strength and potential future weakness. Five years ago, when Thaksin's comment about eighty-five Muslim youngsters who suffocated to death inside military trucks in the southern village of Tak Bai was that "they were already weak from fasting during the month of Ramadan," who could have imagined an old Muslim man from the south praying inside the 1973 monument wearing a T-shirt with Thaksin's face?

A Moment of Relief

I walk away from the memorial and pass the military tanks abandoned by the retreating army on the side of the Italian-sculpted Democracy Monument that ironically portrays soldiers fighting for democracy. I walk towards Sanam Luang and turn left into Tanao Road, passing small groups of red shirts chatting in the shadows. I sit at the end of Khaosan Road, the tourist "ghetto" of Bangkok, on a small step outside a silver shop. To my right are shop windows that were smashed the day before. The shattered pieces are still there. Red shirts and curious onlookers are taking pictures to be archived into people's memories. In front of a Burger King outlet two people were killed. Things have been arranged to transform two blood stains into the last residence of those souls. People with tears in their eyes stare at the bloodstains, delimited by yellow metal barriers and adorned with two dirty red shirts, both with Thaksin's face on them, some flowers and food, rotten in the unbearable heat of the day, and some coins, offerings to the spirits. On the pavement are pieces of stone, food, and the bases of some light poles taken from Ratchdamnoen to be thrown at the army. "They were shot in the head," a young man says to people taking pictures. "Their brains were left on the street pavement." A guy is circling with a pen every bullet hole he can find on the walls. On a big board across the street are pictures of the dead bodies, photographed and reproduced by dozens of cameras, cell phones, and camcorders that will bring them into the private lives of thousands, into their living rooms. Some police officers with bulletproof vests pass by. People search in the rubbish on the side of the road for bullets, memorabilia of this moment. A few meters away, right behind a row of metal barriers delimiting the area, is Khaosan Road. A crowd of young tourists is playing with water. Songkran, the traditional Thai celebration of the new astrological year during which water is poured over Buddha images and then offered to elders to seek their blessings, has evolved over the years into a water-throwing carnival, today celebrated only here.

Thousands of wet underdressed young white kids dance to ear-bursting techno music, throwing water at each other. Their wet clothes stick to their young bodies as they completely ignore what is going on a few meters away. An orgy of adolescent lack of interest, orientalist indifference, and massive disrespect. Some Thai stop for a second, looking at this charade from behind the barriers, wet tanned kids having their battle with buckets and water rifles. Five meters away, I feel disgusted. I realize I should know better and find some social dimension to this, something clever to say, but I just can't, I don't want to, this is simply disgusting. The tourists who were here last week ran away. Those who arrived this week could be kilometers or years away from what is going on beside them.

I sit down in front of a small shop and start writing to get my mind off this scene. Close to me an old man whom I have seen before in this area, one of the many homeless who survive around the tourists, sits staring at the street. His long gray beard falls stiffly on his worn out shirt, and his arms lie relaxed on his thighs. I tell him, "This is crazy." He looks at me, at the "shrines" circling the blood stains. With his hands (I discover he can't speak), he mimes a rifle and a shot in the head. Three barely-dressed British girls pass by, chatting. He turns to me with a big toothless smile and nods in approval, pointing to them and giving me the "ok" with his thumb up. He stands up and follows them into the craziness.

As I sit there, puzzled by the disgust and sense of shame I feel and the old man's attitude, a roar swells from the crowded streets. People start running and shouting in the direction of Democracy Monument. I stand up and pass by the storytellers, who were previously narrating the stories of the fight, now silent. I ask a running woman what is going on. She just says "Dissolution." I leave her behind, enter Ratchadamnoen Avenue, and find a sea of red, cheering, clapping, shouting, and hugging. Everybody is going towards the monument. "The Democrat Party is dissolved," a man shouts. From every street red shirts emerge, joining the river of people. The atmosphere is joyful. You can feel the relief of thousands of people, who arrived from all directions, away from their homes to spend sleepless nights in the heart of the city, and who have been attacked, injured, and shot at just a few days ago. You can feel the release from tension.

I walk again, electrified by the common feeling. People are waving red flags, hands in the sky, as loudspeakers issue the chant, "Democracy is in our hands." I turn to see the silhouettes of people clapping and waving flags, their profiles carved into Ratchadamnoen by a low setting sun at the end of the street. I arrive at the monument. Cheers everywhere. The speakers shout, "One year ago was their Songkran. This year we can celebrate our Songkran, and it will be a Red Songkran!" A young man runs by my side, his arms to the sky, happy. Others around him do the same. Suddenly for a moment, just a very brief moment, everybody seems to pause, as following a silent director. The young man stands, watching Democracy Monument, and starts crying, his mouth distorted. An older man by his side cries as well, but silently. All around people run.

You can see the tension on these faces, the tension of many sleepless nights, the tension of the events of the tenth, portrayed over and over again in the pictures of the dead and injured posted everywhere, now breaking. Red sleepless eyes, bursting into tears. The loudspeakers say it is not over yet, and urge people not to leave. The old man sits down on a chair, nervously looking for his cigarettes, finds the packet and plays with it in his hands, eyes staring at the monument wrapped in red cloth with the words, "Give power back to the people," and beside it the coffins of the dead with their pictures on top. I take some pictures of him and the younger man who is still frozen there, standing, in tears. It is a very powerful moment. I don't know yet what has really happened but seen from here it looks like victory, or at least they need to believe it is. I take some steps, disoriented. An old man walks to me and tells me that one of the dead was a good friend of his, commenting, probably mostly to himself, that now they have not died for nothing but for *chart*, the nation. Another man tells me this is not just for Thailand, but for every person in the world, a demonstration that people have the power, or can claim it.

I go back. The older man still has a packet in his hands. I ask him for a lighter. He passes it to me. I offer to light his cigarette. He says not now and offers me a chair by his side. I sit there for a while in silence. The younger man is not crying anymore. He smiles a smile that you make after a long journey, when you finally breathe. "I haven't slept in three days," the older man tells me, without taking his eyes away from Democracy Monument. "I came to Bangkok exactly thirty days ago for the protest. I had to leave my job." I tell him he will probably sleep well tonight. He laughs. "Will you have a party tonight?" "Not yet," he replies and goes back to torturing his pack of cigarettes. The sensation is overwhelming. People are celebrating. At least for tonight this is going to be the mood.

I walk to Dinso Road where five army tanks are parked. Their interiors have been taken apart, all their weapons removed, and their caterpillar tracks dumped on the street. Anything that could be taken away has been taken away, small mementos of this historic moment. People are jumping on the tanks, trying to find a vantage spot from which to photograph or be photographed. Many kids are standing on top of the armored vehicles as their parents and grandparents take pictures. A man is inside the tank I now stand on, searching for any small part to take away. I take pictures. As many around me, I can't stop taking them at this moment, in front of Democracy Monument standing on a military tank that is covered in messages of democracy, people power, and hatred of the Thai military. On the tank beside me a group of young men are waving red flags. Right behind them, a small crowd is photographing a group of tourists standing on top of another tank, showing their water guns with which they partied in Khaosan until a few minutes ago. Sunset makes the scene more mythical. A motorcycle-taxi guy comes up from the front hole of the tank and sits there, his head out, staring at Democracy Monument. I don't want to ask questions. I want to leave everyone to their own personal moment. An old man asks me to take pictures of him. "I have never seen one of these before," he tells me, mildly embarrassed. You feel on top of the world from here. I get down and take other pictures and discover that the Election Commission has voted to seek the dissolution of the Democrat Party but the issue will still have to go to the Constitutional Court and it won't be fast. Yet people are celebrating as if they won the whole pie. Some sort of relief is needed in these tense days, and this decision offers the occasion.

I walk down the street. Again people are taking pictures with the tanks. "Fuck Thai Army" is written on one of them in English. Down the road, two military jeeps have crashed on the street, blocking the way. A few meters away, another is turned on its side. Beyond them is the normal life of Bangkok, as if nothing has happened. I get back on Ratchadamnoen, the same atmosphere of festivity, people clapping, cheering, and hugging. Many people just sit, alone, soaking in the moment as night conquers the sky. Some people leave but the protest slowly resumes. Motorcycle-taxis zip everywhere, diffusing people and good news across the city.

INSIGHTFUL, IN TREND, INDEPENDENT

THE NATION

THAILAND WEDNESDAY, April 14, 2010

Byron, Cindy Bishop on raising a baby

THE RIGHT TYPE OF FIGHT

FIGHTING breaks out on Khao San Road – with water guns – as locals and foreign visitors both in the city and countryside brave temperatures in the 40s to enjoy the Songkran festival yesterday. Tourist numbers on Khao San Road were reportedly up to 30 per cent even though only a few days have elapsed since the violent clashes in the neighbourhood. The red-shirted protesters also celebrated the traditional Thai New Year inside their base camp.

However, 43 countries have issued warnings to their citizens about travelling to the Kingdom during the political volatility. China and Japan have banned or advised against all tour groups to Bangkok until further notice.

Annual water festival kicks off in a relatively good atmosphere.

Banharn to PM: Decide soon on House dissolution, charter

'PM NOT STEPPING DOWN'

SATURDAY'S CLASHES

THEIR MAJESTIES TO PAY MEDICAL BILLS

Graciously cover treatment for all injured in April 10 violence, and funeral subsidy

Their Majesties the King and Queen will graciously cover the medical bills for victims of Saturday's clash between troops and red-shirted demonstrators.

The Office of His Majesty's Principal Private Secretary yesterday said hospitals and agencies had been notified about Their Majesties' concern and their intent to pay for treatment.

A MOTHER tends her son, a soldier who was wounded in last Saturday's clashes, at the Army's Phra Mongkut Klao hospital yesterday. Donations of food and money have been flooding into the hospital.

sit on the western side of Democracy Monument. Boxes that were lying around yesterday, scattered on the pavement, have been organized in blocks, and thousands of different hands have written their own messages on them: objections to the government, questions about the government or other institutions and their roles, or whatever they wanted to say, most of the time in Thai, occasionally in English. These boxes have been transformed into a massive blackboard for people to express themselves. An older artist collected some money from friends with this idea in mind and brought the boxes to the street a few days ago. Today, the beginning of the proper Songkran celebrations that will run for the next two days, he and a group of collaborators have rearranged them, creating a wall that almost covers a side of the monument. The boxes have been attached to each other with iron mesh and fixed with red ropes attached to nails hammered into the monument's pavement. A group of three artists have started drawing on top of the messages a massive Democracy Monument in black, leaning on one side, a symbol of what they see as the ongoing destruction of democracy in Thailand.

In the middle of the street dotted with people, covered by the thin shadow cast by the monument, a young artist starts drawing the outline, comparing the proportions of his lines with the monument behind the cartoon wall. Two old couples stop to stare, puzzled. The older artist, wearing a white hat from which gray hair pops out on the sides, inspects the work and at times picks up a brush to correct, with firm hands, the outlines drawn by his young helper. Soon a small crowd gathers, sitting on the asphalt, using the little shadow cast by cars parked around as protection from the burning sun. One man in his fifties sits close to me and asks where I am from. We start talking. He tells me that he participated in buying the boxes and bringing them here. He says that people started writing on them on the tenth, after the helicopters flew over the area and dropped tear gas on the crowd. The boxes were laid out around the monument only the day after. He asks me how to translate "Abolish aristocracy" into English and walks to the painter with the piece of paper I wrote on. The monument behind, the real one, has been wrapped in a multicolored piece of cloth, with a red wrapping at the top and a huge red cloth around the monument saying, "Give power back to the people."

As the shadows cast by the cars parked in the empty roundabout grow, more people gather to watch the emerging painting. A young girl passes by with a leaking water gun. A couple in Hawaiian red shirts with white flowers stamped on them take pictures. The young painter applies thick layers of black paint. He is in his twenties, wearing a black T-shirt, jeans, and black sunglasses. Behind him the voice of a man directs people through three lines of monks and older people seated on chairs on the northern side of the monument, there to receive Songkran water offerings. The monks' ochre robes lend another shade to the scene. Red shirts walk through the lines pouring small quantities of water into the monks' hands holding orchid flowers, pass to a lower line of seated elders, and then come up above them to pour water on a golden Buddha image. The Songkran atmosphere at Ratchadamnoen is very different from that at Ratchaprasong. There, younger crowds throw water at each other in the street, mixing with foreigners to the sound of loud pop music. No offering to elders. A large dance party fills the intersection at Pratunam. Back in Ratchadamnoen, at the beginning of Dinso Road, people crowd around the parked military tanks which have also been transformed by boards for red shirts' political messages. A young father lifts his small child up to sit on a tank, and takes a picture as the kid looks around, lost, his red head band calling for dissolution. Behind him the tanks swarm with people trying to break off the few remaining detachable parts to bring home.

On the eastern side of the monument, the red-painted coffins of people who died on Saturday lie on tables. Long lines of people wait to have a moment in front of the coffins or to chat briefly and give support to the relatives of the dead, who stand in front of the wooden boxes, pictures of their loved ones held tightly in their hands. A voice behind them, coming from the stage at Phan Fa Bridge, says ironically, "We are very lucky to have Abhisit as our prime minister." Each coffin is covered in flowers and bears a picture of the body inside and a copy of his or her national ID. Names, faces, ages, addresses, forever inscribed in the memories of many. The lines of people coming for a gaze, a picture, or a hand placed on the coffins just for a second seem endless. On the pavement, also covered with handwriting, hundreds of incense sticks burn in three big jars. On the sidewalks other long lines of people gather around a stall registering people as signed-up members of UDD and giving them an ID card. This seems to be one evident short-term effect of the military attack. Interminable lines of silent people waiting to be photographed and receive a red-shirt membership card. Many of them have been at the protest for weeks but only now have decided to get formal membership to the movement. Three or four stalls along Ratchadamnoen Avenue serve this mass of people. They pay fifty baht for the plastic card holder, complete a paper form, and wait for hours to be put in front of a red backdrop and a digital camera, before receiving their plastic card, for another hundred baht. Inside the stalls, four or five young supporters sit in front of laptops and small tripods with digital cameras, volunteering their time in this seemingly endless operation of recording names and faces. The attack that was supposed to instill fear and despair seems to have created a stronger push to be formally involved. "We won't go home until we win," an old man tells me, his wrinkles creasing into a sunburned smile. Behind him a young couple pretend to be fighting among themselves, as a young woman giggles. A few steps away, a kid plays with a small plastic water gun, following a dog. Beside them, an old motorcycle-taxi driver waits silently in line, his orange vest adding another tone of color to the scene. On one side, small groups of people help each other to fill in the form correctly, passing pens along to the next in line. Thailand's humanity fills these lines, silently waiting to document their political participation. On the opposite side of the monument a single piece of white cloth hangs from a scaffolding, bearing just one eloquent word in red: "SAD," in English.

On the making of history

As the first days after the violence go by, histories are being created, told, and retold in the two streets around Democracy Monument from which the army attack came: Dinso Road, a big street on the northern side of the monument, and Tanao Road at the end of Khaosan Road, the backpackers' mecca of Bangkok. Both streets are slowly entering the mythology of this protest, its conceptual and photographic memories.

Tanao Road, where I have spent most of my time in the last few days, was one of the first streets built in Bangkok, when most citizens moved about on water. It now crosses the newer Ratchadamnoen Avenue a few hundred meters west of Democracy Monument. On the other side of the avenue, Tanao Road is much larger, but it narrows on this side, providing the perfect bottleneck for a military crackdown. I came here the day after the violence and wrote a bit. The street exudes an eerie feeling. Small shrines for the dead have been set up on the pavement, overflowing with objects—pieces of clothes, candles, coins and other donations. A few steps away, rubbish covers the street's corners, pieces of stone coming from who knows where, and bases of streetlamps from nearby streets. Overlooking this scene, behind iron barriers, are *farang* tourists throwing water at each other. People stroll around, bending forward, searching through the rubbish for bullets or other portable memorabilia of the violence. Slowly, their numbers grow, all looking around in almost religious silence. Most of them are well-dressed, not in red shirts but with a red scarf or a wristband, easy to take off once they leave the area, clear signs of less strong affiliation and belonging to a certain class. These are not the people who were here during the confrontation. In the silence, broken by the strident music coming from Khaosan Road, cameras everywhere capture histories. As the flow of people searching for a piece of history grows, a big board goes up in the middle of the street, hanging from red ropes attached to the street lamps. On this board are glued a series of sixteen photographs, the same fast-printed ones that are to appear everywhere in the protest areas. At street corners, inside shops, on the monument, on car windows, on the walls, these gruesome images are proliferating, printed and sold around the city for a few baht in stalls equipped with small printers.

People start gathering in front of the board when Seh Daeng (the nickname of Khattiya Sawasdipol), a popularly acclaimed army general turned red-shirt leader, appears from the end of the street. He walks with a small entourage of guards in combat jackets. He checks the photos first, stands there visibly touched, and salutes with a *wai* the two "shrines" on the street. Walking away, he stops to stare at a shattered shop window behind a closed metal cover. He runs his hands over the shop's walls, deciphering bullet holes for the crowd. "M16," he says and the small crowd around him mutters in Thai: "*em sip hok.*" All of this small inspection is done with the utmost calm, almost with grace. People in the crowd cheer and try to get a picture with him. Later I have to force my ears to remember the noise and the clapping of plastic feet. Staring at him my brain somehow stores the moment as a silent one, even if only a few meters away techno music is playing at full volume. As he moves away to the middle of the street to allow the crowd to record and take away his photos and words, a middle-aged man, dressed in rather odd skateboarder-like style, pulls out a red marker from his black backpack and starts circling the bullet holes in the Burger King's window, different from the ones Seh Daeng checked, and far too big and deep to be from an M16. A circle, an arrow, a few words, repeated at every bullet hole.

The sun goes down and dusk descends on the small road. A larger crowd arrives, attracted by the spreading news about the presence of Seh Daeng, who has already left. The skeletons of cars and taxis, drilled by bullets, parked on the street on the tenth to block the advance of the army, lie in the dim light. Some people emerge from the crowd and stand in front of the shrines or the pictures, retelling the events of recent days. Two men take the central stage between the board and the shrines: a young man, who looks like he has been sleeping around here for a while, in a torn red shirt, and an old man, toothless and without shoes. They recount confused and often inconsequential stories, trying to catch and retain the eyes of the crowd. They both say they were here and saw people fall. The young guy, the one I follow more closely, speaks about the events in a detached tone, as a tour guide. "The army came from there," he says pointing to the road behind the cars. "But they were also on top of the buildings. The red shirts pushed back and forth, back and forth, and then the soldiers started shooting and they had weapons. They were using weapons against people with bare hands." A woman in the crowd asks if the people died there, pointing with her eyes to the small shrine, right beside the man. The guy says honestly, "I don't know if they died here or there. Everybody was pushing back and forth. It could have been there." His eyes rove around for a second. Another *farang* asks in English if the Japanese reporter was killed here. Somebody translates and the speaker says again that it is not easy to tell, there was a big confusion, it may even have been on another street. No personal pictures are placed by the blood stains, just some food, some coins, and two torn red shirts with the sad face of Thaksin in white.

A flow of water from Khaosan Road slowly inundates the red shrines. History is in the making, cold enough for the curious, the well-dressed red shirts, the "military leaders," for the pictures, the collections and the close but undisturbed Songkran celebration, but still too warm to take a definite form. Histories on the dark street are still fluid and open to interpretation. The guy with the marker, the comments from Seh Daeng, the objects that people were putting on the shrines—everything is imploding and converging into a more fixed version of history, a history of violence and sacrifice, of state repression and personal heroism, a history that will be challenged and sometime even completely denied by state propaganda and mass media, but will be retold, in personal conversations and VCD screenings at the protest and in thousands and thousands of houses throughout the country.

On April 14, I go back again in the late afternoon. The mood is quite different. Many more people, mostly young, carrying water rifles crowd the street, attracted more by the "traditional" wet dance party of Songkran in Khaosan Road than by the call of history. Most of them, however, stop to check out a picture board towering in the middle of the street. Using the board as a teacher would use a blackboard, a man in a red shirt has become the official storyteller in the area. One after the other, people arrive, stare at the macabre pictures, take some pictures of pictures, often with their cell phones, and walk on, towards or away from the water. The storyteller keeps going, restarting again and again, going through the pictures showing the photo of the guy who was killed precisely where we stand. As soon as I stop there to listen, another guy grabs my arm. "You don't have to pay for this," he tells me and starts retelling the events, cutting straight to the part that he thinks foreigners are interested in: the Japanese reporter's death. He tells me that the second stain, the one more inside Tanao Road, is where the Japanese reporter died. "Look, there is also a Japanese flag," he says as he points with his finger to the small flag that appeared there yesterday in a bamboo vase full of rotting roses. I turn around and ask him, "Was it scary?" ready to receive the classic boastful response. "I don't know," he answers, "I wasn't here the night of the tenth." I keep walking down the road past cars that block the street, every window smashed into glass spiderwebs by bullet holes. I stand in front of them, trying to get a picture.

After the sunlight has completely gone, a mildly overweight man in his forties, black ruffled hair, white oxford shirt with blue stripes, a black backpack, thick eyeglasses, and a very big red scarf around his neck, stands with a motorcycle-taxi driver, an old man with a carved face and two thick brush strokes of the white talcum powder used during Songkran on his cheeks. As the driver starts telling the story of what happened, an old woman comes out of an alley and joins the group, followed by a young woman and an even younger boy. Three generations listening. I get closer. They are speaking about the direction of the shots. The driver is talking of twenty snipers on top of a big white building, shooting into the crowd. He pulls out of his pocket a picture of the guy left brainless, a picture which now is at the top of every board in the protest area, as proof that the bullets arrived from above. The man with the scarf asks if the red side had weapons. The driver pauses for a second, shrugs his shoulders and says, "Yeah, sure, some had weapons, but I did not see anyone using them." Then he points with his head to the direction of the shrines and asks the man if he wants to go there. "We have already seen it," answers the young woman, in a conversation that resembles those with tourist guides. The driver turns and tells me to go and see. Almost unconsciously I follow his advice. When I realize that I am going back, I retrace my steps but it is too late. They are gone.

Only twenty-four hours later, history is crystallizing into a less fluid form. Blood stains are given names, faces, and paraphernalia to add strength to the narration. A small Japanese flag, a picture of the brainless body, a hole in the wall. History is in the making, a history of events and people, a small localized history that works as an appendix to the big history that particular events can change, as the red shirts hope they will.

wake up to news that red shirts are dismantling the protest at Democracy Monument and moving completely to the Ratchaprasong area. I get in a cab and arrive at Phan Fa Bridge, which is now reachable even by car. The intersection is empty. The stage is still there. A few people are collecting garbage and taking down tents. A man stands alone on the stripped-down stage, singing. Traffic is back, but very light. In front of Wat Ratchanatda, overlooked by the Golden Mountain, small empty shelters made of plastic sheets and sticks wave in the morning wind. Some people are taking apart the white stalls that occupied the sides of Ratchadamnoen and storing the material in large trucks, ready to be rebuilt again down Ratchadamri Road. In the sleepy atmosphere of the morning, small groups of people are taking apart everything that the red shirts had built in the area.

As I arrive at Democracy Monument, the three artists who built the cardboard box wall a few days ago are also dismantling it, carefully folding the boxes. The man who directed the work greets me. I sit there for a moment as the temperature rises. I take some pictures and find myself helping them store the boxes. The guy is wearing a light blue T-shirt, darkened by spots of sweat. He gives me a pair of pliers to cut the iron mesh that connects the boxes, and starts telling me that the older man, the only artist among them, has been doing public art since 1976. He and the other man helping out were student activists during that time. They both studied for some years (one year in his case) at Thammasat University and went into the jungle after the October 6 massacre of students. He was in Isan for three years, his friend was in Phitsanulok (a province in lower northern Thailand). As we keep working under a relentless sun, everybody around is taking things apart, packing up objects, moving away in cars. Two motorcycle-taxi drivers give last tours of the occupied monument, pointing to pictures still standing, followed by a small group of people walking through the red coffins, now stripped of flowers and flags. Just four pieces of wood in red on the pavement in an empty square. It is stunning how fast things can change. On our left, a huge burial structure was built to burn the coffins if and when the government resigned. A trolley is parked there as a dozen people take down the structure, maybe to be rebuilt elsewhere.

The older artist, Phi Leek, who has been collecting his other paintings printed on plastic sheets from the monument, comes back and greets me distractedly. He has the slim face and dried body of old people who have always been active. Soft hands. A few white strings of beard sprout from his chin and white hair peeps from the sides of a once white, now yellowish, hat. He wears a large white shirt, beige pants, and flip-flops. I ask him about Thai Artists for Freedom, the group that signed all the works of art on the monument. "It is just me," he says, half-smiling, "I have been doing this for a long time, on the side, with other forms of art as well, more or less political. I collect money from friends and use it to put up art at political protests." He speaks with a soft voice, words slipping away from his missing teeth. I ask him if I can call him and talk more. He tells me that I must go to his house, as he stays there and comes to protests only if he has something to do. We go back to work while some of the people helping sit in the shade, taking a break. I get close to Nit, the man I talked to before. He points to a single woman's shoe left in the street and suggests that I put it underneath me as the pavement is burning. I sit with him, balancing on the shoe. Soon he starts talking about 1976 and his experience as a student then. "We students at that time were the people talking, the people on stage, but at the end it was the normal people, the workers that really made up the movement." He looks around at the street where many of his friends were killed, forcing him to leave university and live in the forest for three years. He tells me that in 1976 the government recruited people from the countryside as the infamous "village scouts" to fight against the students and the people protesting. "Now those villagers are part of the red shirts." He pauses for a moment. "The same people who killed us are now protesting here, at our side." In the silence before he stands up and goes back to work, I think that history has a weird way of repeating itself. Common enemies create odd friendships, especially if the past is painfully carved in your mind.

We finally manage to organize the empty boxes and drive to Ratchaprasong in his wide jeep, full of folded boxes from the wall. Other folded boxes are on top of the car, increasing its height. We drive through Siam Square where people have fully occupied the sidewalks in front of Siam Paragon, laid down their mats, and started rebuilding shelters for the coming nights. A vendor of grilled chicken, who two nights ago was filling the roundabout of Democracy Monument with smoke, is setting up shop in a new, again carefully chosen, location at the corner of Siam Square. We drive through a flock of people walking, sitting, busily setting up shops, raising shelters, and building stalls. At the corner with Henry Dunant Road we get stopped by a red-shirt traffic controller, one of the hundreds of guards who manage access and security at entrances to the protest areas. Nit explains to him that we are coming to put up an art piece in front of Siam Paragon. The guard, a man in his forties with a gray T-shirt and bushy eyebrows, tells him that he must go the other way if he is aiming for Siam Paragon. "Central World," I tell him. He looks at us, confused, and mutters something into a black walkie-talkie. Nit pulls out his camera to show pictures of the boxes. The guard takes a look at the pictures and tells us we cannot pass through as there are too many people in the street now. I ask if Pratunam could be better and he nods, "Go ask there," deflecting responsibility. Guards are the same no matter what color they wear.

We drive into Henry Dunant Road, make a U-turn, and with the power of the driver's red shirt we pass another roadblock and drive back into Rama I Road. The street is swarming with people, pickups, *tuk-tuk*s, cars, taxis, and especially the ubiquitous motorcycle-taxis, soon to be the only means of transportation available in the area and capable of traversing the crowd, allowing mobility to people on and off the protest as well as in its belly. A horde of people and vehicles seems to be coming towards us. We somehow manage to move against the current. Nit is talking to me about his job as an editor of *D-Magazine*, one of the many journals, newspapers, and other red publications that are circulating. "Too much competition," he says, smiling. "We have finished the money and we are at risk of going out of business." He switches subjects and asks me about the Communist Party in Italy, criticizing the Maoist direction of the Communist Party of Thailand and other institutional forces in Thailand. We drive back to Ratchathewi Road, where a motorcycle-taxi driver with a whistle directs the traffic. At the intersection with Petchaburi Road I tell Nit, "You should turn right but you have to go straight and take a U-tur..." "We are red," he interrupts me with a smile. "We can turn right here." He cuts across three lanes and turns to shout politely to a policeman inside the booth, "Wehavetodropsomethingthankyou" with no pause. The traffic is now unbearable so he drops me off and goes straight onto the flyover, towards Onnut, abandoning the plan to deposit the boxes today. I walk to Pratunam. The street here is packed, as a river of people makes its way into the protest site. On the small bridge at Pratunam, vendors sell buckets full of white powder and water guns, cashing in on the Songkran celebrations. Beside them, functioning as a border of the protest, a group of young Thai listen to hard rock music, pounding at full volume from black speakers on the back of a pickup. Completely covered with white powder, their young bodies dance to the rhythm of the music in an ecstatic mix of water, heat, and loud noise. I pass them carefully so as not to get my camera wet and walk into the protest.

The crowd has grown significantly since the evacuation of Phan Fa Bridge but the extent of the protest area remains the same. As a consequence the density of people is much higher, and growing. I walk up onto an overpass to take pictures of the red sea from above. In the direction of Central World the face of a popular Thai movie star looms over the crowd on an advertisement board. He is carrying a camera that flashes every fifteen seconds or so. On the other side, three young models look down from huge advertisement boards at the dancing crowd. The three sisters carry the names Gucci, Louis Vuitton, and Versace. On the overpass I bump into another book vendor of classic leftist books. I have met him many times already at protests and at conferences at a local university. He greets me warmly and asks me how often I come to the protest. "Every day since I got back," I answer. "Every day for me too," he replies, "for two weeks." He is sitting on a motorbike, wearing a green,

Mao-like cap with a red star on his forehead, a red shirt, and jeans. In front of him on a plastic table covered with blue cloth are his books. We start talking about the protest and the clearing of the other site. I ask him why they decided to move here. "The owners of these shopping malls are the people behind this government and the aristocracy. They don't want the army to engage in any fight here. That will damage their property." We look around for a second. "We are safer here, protected by Louis Vuitton bags," he laughs. This place of exclusion, a material symbol of unequal access to resources, has been transformed into a shelter for the red-shirt movement, precariously protected by a shield of jewels and luxury goods. "They have no problem in destroying lives but they don't want to destroy goods," he says out loud. Around us, red-shirt protesters keep buying from the many street vendors: food, beverages, T-shirts, wristbands, clappers, flip-flops, pictures, DVDs.

We start talking about politics and I ask him why the students are not present in this protest. "They are," he replies. "Not too many," I say. He stops for a second "Since '76, students have not been too involved in politics. You know, students now are interested in the good life, in partying. This is not a protest of the students; it is a protest of the people, which is much better. The people now don't need students to teach them. Earlier, the students thought they knew and understood but in the end they had their own ideas and dreams. Now the people can speak for themselves. This is the main change." I ask him about the yellow shirts. "What do you think they think? Why do they support what you call a dictatorship?" He looks at me and makes me feel as if it was a stupid question. "TV, the media, they all create an idea. Yellow shirts believe Thaksin is bad and so anything that comes with him is bad. You know, I don't like Thaksin either," he says, lowering his tone, voicing a position that is slowly spreading, "but now it is clear Thaksin was just a tool. This is not about him anymore. I didn't like him. But he had good policies."

He starts telling me about his first born, of his young pregnant wife being able to give birth for only thirty baht, against the fifty thousand baht that a friend of theirs spent in a private hospital. As we talk my eyes fall on the books. I ask him, "Which books do you sell more? What are people buying?" "*Fa Diao Kan* [Same Sky], another journal called *An* [Reading], and the books of Jit Phumisak." "Are people reading Marx or Lenin?" I ask, pointing to Marx's beard dominating two covers. "Some— the people who are interested in political thought." I tell him that I never understood the relationship between red shirts and communist symbolism. The question makes him uncomfortable and he starts to be defensive, maybe as a reaction to years of propaganda equating communists with enemies of the state. "Red shirts are not communists," he starts out. The Maoist hat on his head seems to disagree. "There are some former communists, Maoists, who are in red shirts but they understand that both communism and this movement are about democracy first." He seems to lean for a more socialist position, looking at Pridi Banomyong as an example. "So what next if the government is dissolved?" "The red shirts should create a new party and maybe also the yellow shirts should create a new party so as to have a real bipartisan system." We talk for a while about Thai society and the welfare state in Europe. Not everyone in the crowd wants to talk for hours about politics. I say goodbye and walk away. The light of day is almost gone, blocked by the imposing buildings above us.

The large plaza in front of Central World swarms with people, each person finding his or her own space for the night and for the coming days. People are moving in an endless flow. Some walk with chairs, some lay mats, some park their carts, renegotiating space among the protesters who have been here for the last few weeks and the newcomers. The protest now extends well down Ratchadamri Road, almost reaching Lumphini Park. Slowly the white stalls that were at Ratchadamnoen Avenue are being put up along the street. I hop on a motorcycle-taxi, too tired to walk another step. On the way home I talk with the driver, who comes every day from Thonburi, on the other side of the river, to be part of the movement and make some money on the side. He asks me how much I would have agreed to pay for this ride if I did not know the normal price, testing the water for the next *farang* who hails him.

wake up in the morning and go directly to Siam Square, zigzagging through the traffic that stagnates at the frontiers of the protest. U-turn in Silom Road, passing through the barrier that separates the two lanes, and turn left into Thaniya Road, full of prostitutes and Japanese restaurants during the night but empty and asleep till noon. Park in Siam Square. All around, small groups of police officers wear orange and purple scarves to differentiate units. Rama I Road has been transformed into a pedestrian walkway, sheltered by the imposing cement structures of the Skytrain. Huge white stalls occupy the two sides of the street, leaving a narrow path for people and slow-moving motorcycle-taxis. A shirtless old man takes a nap in the intense heat. Vendors fill the sidewalks and part of the street with food and a multitude of red merchandise: wristbands, T-shirts, flip-flops with the face of Abhisit and Suthep, scarves, stickers, flags, pictures, CDs of the protests, tapes of speeches, the ubiquitous clappers with red feet, jackets with POLICE written on them. On my right, Thaksin jumps out of a tall poster, dressed in clothes from the movie, *The Matrix*, two guns in his hands. As I pass through this river of objects, my visual, olfactory, and sonic senses go into overdrive. On my right, at the FARED (First Aid Red Shirts) stall, where volunteers, mostly middle-aged women, distribute first aid and free pills for different kinds of health problems, an international media conference is taking place.

A small crowd of foreign journalists is surrounded by Thai of all ages, separated from them by a red plastic cordon and listening, often without understanding the mixture of Thai and English. At the end of the stall, a large white table hosts a professor of Chulalongkorn University, a former yellow shirt who, as she puts it, came to her senses after the coup and joined the red movement; a monk, who briefly spoke at the end about nonviolence; and two other people I don't recognize. Behind them, as in a strange police lineup, stand three women and a man, each with a large framed picture of a relative killed on April 10. One of the women carries a forensic picture of her son, lifeless. The youngest of the four is probably thirteen or fourteen years old, her silent eyes looking forward but glued to the ground, her small hands clinging to a picture of someone who may have been her father, similar faces and identical noses. He is wearing a large cowboy hat, and his eyes look very serious and mildly sad. Everyone in that row looks trapped behind the table, conscious of being observed. They try not to meet others' eyes. They do not say a word. All of them wear red shirts. An older woman with short black hair in a black oxford shirt is acting as the MC, facilitating interventions and explaining in English and then in Thai the next step, as well as introducing the speakers. I stand behind another red cordon that divides the stage space of the stall from the audience space, filled with journalists scribbling notes or filming what is going on. I start talking with a few of them about recent events. A female Thai freelance journalist, working as a facilitator for the foreign press, listens to our conversation, commenting now and then. A young man gets the microphone and loudly relates what happened to him on April 10. His car was among those parked in Tanao Road to block the advance of the army. As he was parking the car, he was shot at with rubber bullets, smashing his car's windows. He was then taken out of the car, beaten on the street, and brought to a military camp for five hours of interrogation and beating. Even in English he speaks like people on stage, changing the inflection and the volume of his speech for emphasis. The red shirts around read the clues carefully, even without understanding what he is saying, clapping every time his voice rises, maybe an automatic reaction after so many days of being bombarded with the rhythm of political tirades. I walk away, disturbed by this thought.

The atmosphere at the protest is tense. Usually, during the hot hours, the area is quite empty, with a few people clustered around the stage, often sitting on their motorcycles or in any place with shade, gathering along the walls of the shopping malls, using the small tongue of shadow cast by the enormous complexes, or underneath the three overpasses that cross Ratchadamri Road. Today, something is different. The crowds are unusually sparse, the music is playing more softly, the security is tighter on the whole perimeter where motorcycles are stopped and their seats checked. Rumors are running around of another imminent attack by the army. There is a strange feeling of a calm before the storm, of tenseness waiting for an upcoming meeting between the army chiefs, and for the decisions that will be taken. In the meantime, the red shirts are raising the stakes, announcing they will extend the protest to the Silom area, the financial heart of the city. The army's response to this was short and rapid. An army spokesman announced on camera that this will not be permitted and that the "mob will not be allowed to be flexible anymore." On another square of this psychological chess board, on the other side of town at Rangsit University, the yellow shirts are meeting, hoping to come up with a plan, or some sort of platform to voice their opinion. Later today, they will join the "no-color" protests at Victory Monument and give the government a seven-day deadline to resolve the situation with the reds or else they will intervene directly as concerned citizens. It is a day of pause, staring into the enemy's eyes, strategizing, and talking of conspiracy and movements of soldiers on the roofs above Ratchaprasong, all of this under a cover of calm and restraint. The antagonists, how many of them it is difficult to say, ponder their next move.

All across the city, political discussions are raging in homes, streets, and shops. I get out of the house to buy some food and return a movie. Passing in front of the 7-Eleven at the corner of my *soi*, I'm stopped by a motorcycle-taxi driver, who has transformed his vest into a moving board scribbled with messages against dictatorship. He talks fast in a mixture of Thai and political terms in English. From the basket in front of his motorbike, he pulls a piece of paper from a thick brown envelope. He tells me to read it, asking that I read the first line as proof of my ability to read Thai. The short page explains the basic political concepts of democratic systems: popular rule, legitimacy, parliament. "I wrote it myself," he explains proudly, "to explain politics to the Thai people who do not understand what the difference is between parliamentary and dictatorial systems and believe they have democracy when they don't." He speaks very fast, constantly interrupting his own speech to ask me about the system in Italy and about Mussolini. I ask him if he supports the red shirts. He tells me it is a step forward. He supports them but is looking for revolution, not reform. He greets a young woman and gives her a copy of the pamphlet. I say goodbye and walk away, passing two women returning home from their office in yellow T-shirts.

As announced, the army has moved into the Silom area, securing it against any expansion of the red shirts' protest. I wake up and try to get a sense of the news of the day, struggling to find independent websites and blogs not blocked by state censorship. Frustrated, I head to Ratchaprasong, hoping to use my eyes to fill the blank created by repression. I enter from Pratunam. Nobody checks me so I ride to the half-empty intersection, almost reaching the stage. Where the cardboard box wall used to stand, a mime sits in the sun, white painted face and red clothes, immobile. The reds have stretched a long plastic cloth to cover the area between the stage and the first overpass. On the overpass at Silom subway station, soldiers have unfurled a similar cloth to cover their movements and to control the red shirts standing across the street. The long dark green cloth in Ratchaprasong makes the passage from the road to the shaded area refreshing. In a few steps the temperature drops significantly. A small crowd stands or sits on motorcycles, listening to a speaker talking about the motorcycle-taxi drivers, taxi drivers, and street vendors who have been at the protest, forsaking their income to be here. All of these workers, according to my discussions with them, are on the contrary making good money at the protest. I sit here for a while, enjoying the cool, and then ride away down Ratchadamri Road, reduced to a small stretch surrounded by twenty-meter-long white tents: pharmacy, dormitory of the people from Pattaya, Surin, Saraburi, another pharmacy, speakers, video station, monks' tents, kitchen. I pass a fifty- or sixty-meter-long queue of people waiting to get their red-shirt ID card. I drive to the head of the protest in front of Lumphini Park, where the red shirts and the army officers face each other in the heat, divided by Rama IV Road, crowded as usual by the traffic flow.

On the red side, a barricade of big flower boxes has been erected. Behind this, from a set of loudspeakers on the back of a truck, a young woman's voice invites the protesters to be calm and let the soldiers do their job, calling them "brothers military." Beside the truck a small crowd of red shirts, mostly tough looking men carrying sharpened bamboo sticks, loiter around, emanating a pungent smell of rice whiskey. I sit there for a while, watching them shouting at the army on the other side of the street, through the chaotic traffic on Rama IV Road. I start talking with a young man who has been here since yesterday afternoon, sleeplessly waiting for the army to attack. His red eyes glimmer in the sun as many around him move piles of bamboo sticks and motorcycle helmets, pathetic defense tools against the army rifles pointed at them from the subway overpass. Behind this movement, a number of motorcycle-taxis, ready to relay updates from this front to the leaders in case anything happens, sit there enjoying the show. On the other side of the barricades, talking through the spaces between flowerpots, six motorcycle-taxi drivers, sitting on their bikes, report to the protesters the numbers, equipment, and location of the army personnel.

I grab my bike and cross into Silom Road, passing through a small gate still open on a side of Lumphini Park. The street is very quiet. Small crowds of citizens on both sides of the street are waiting to see what is going to happen or just taking pictures of this military deployment. The financial district is peppered with small groups of soldiers in full war gear, protective vests and pads, and heavy weapons. Many more soldiers hide in the small alleys: lounging, sitting, waiting. A crowd of young men, barely bearded, sit between buildings, carrying war weaponry. Here and there, fifteen or twenty rifles lean against the wall. Outside the army lines, police officers in anti-riot gear control the situation. I ride to the Narathiwat intersection, park my bike, and go by foot to take pictures. Several small groups of military sit or hide in the *sois* with rifles, M16s, and other automatic guns, sometimes in their hands, sometimes left in a pile while the troops nap in the midday heat. Kids. Confused kids for the most part, dressed as puppets with rifles too big and too deadly to be put in to their hands.

Inside Patpong Road, the main sex street of the city, stands a big contingent of soldiers, commanded by an older man sitting on a military jeep with big speakers on top. Another group sits on the opposite side, underneath the entrance to a strip club called Safari. Judging from the weapons they carry compared to those of their enemy, this operation could well be some sort of safari. The yellow-on-black lettering on the club's signboard glimmers in the sun like the young privates' camouflage uniforms: Safari. The weapons casually draped on their shoulders confirm: Safari.

Privates and prostitutes go way back in Thailand, since the Vietnam War, happy to sustain each other's business. An old woman emerges from a half-closed door, bringing some water to a soldier. Another soldier, seated on a high stool, displays his weapons, excited by the attention of my camera. As I walk down Silom Road, I notice a mass of roses and plastic bags full of goods lying close to the soldiers. Some women in their thirties wearing office clothes, oxford shirts and short skirts or long pants, black or gray, go around distributing bags from 7-Eleven filled with snacks and drinks for the soldiers, who thank them with a *wai* and an extra look as the group walks away. These women are not alone. Other groups, always composed of young women, distribute bags of drinks or coffee, for the visual and voiced gratitude of the young military. As in the morning almsgiving to monks, donations are made along gender lines. Here the donors are moving, not the receivers.

Soldiers and red shirts face each other from afar through the sound of traffic, unbearably hot under their protective clothing, the smell of street food in their nostrils, and with the same sleep-deprived red eyes. Eye to eye, not just soldiers and red shirts, but two faces of Thailand, two different ways of conceiving the role of citizen and social being. On one side, an idea of social responsibility and citizenship that stresses order, respect for a chain of command, and compassion and generosity towards the state and its leaders, who are there for everybody's good. Such a citizen *wai*s to the soldiers, brings them food and drinks *phuea chat*, for the nation, to celebrate and support its brave defenders. On the other side, an idea of citizenship based on participation, watching closely the state and its governors, of being Thai and working for the good of the nation, *phuea chat*, by revolting against a system perceived as unjust and to be changed "for the future of the country," as an old man said today, almost spitting it out through his front teeth. These two Thailands are today silently facing each other across Rama IV Road, both armed with conviction, certain of being in the right, but carrying different weapons— sticks and slingshots against steel tools of war. In this reciprocal gaze there is much of recent Thai history, a history of class and regional conflict, of obedience and "moderation," of burning ideals and fearless protests, all these parallel histories reflected through the same red eyes of youths from lower income families. The same exact eyes on both sides, the country looking at itself.

I walk back on the overpass. Here the number of soldiers is overwhelming, battery after battery of men napping on the pavement beside overflowing piles of goods and plastic bags donated by people. This is a "yellow area" after all. At the entrance of the Sala Daeng Skytrain station a small group of soldiers sits chatting while an endless line of soldiers sleep on the pavement beside them. In the background, zen music is blessing this absurd vision. I get off and try in vain to talk to some soldiers who predictably reply that they cannot talk or that they are just following orders, an old excuse. I walk to the end of Silom Road where a half-destroyed building has become some sort of headquarters for the operation. Inside, there are two or three older officers at a large table, a street vendor selling food, and many bags disposed on the ground very carefully, too carefully not to contain anything dangerous. For the first time I am asked by one of the officers not to take pictures. The building at the corner between Silom and Narathiwat Road is surrounded by wire mesh. Soldiers stand at each entry, in pairs. Inside, three motorcycle-taxi drivers talk to military officers. I guess everybody has their motorcycle-taxi informants. As a driver told me, they are the "owners of the map" after all.

After resting at home, I go back to Ratchaprasong in the evening to meet a young Thai documentary maker at McDonalds in Amarin Plaza, hoping to be there at the protest to see the reactions to Abhisit's interview on Channel 9 at 11:00 p.m. The filmmaker is sitting inside McDonalds with three other friends, a small packet of French fries on the table. The four have been sitting there for at least two hours, a usual way to use air-conditioned space in Bangkok. We sit there for a moment and then go out looking for a TV. There are many sets in the area but none turned to the prime minister's interview. We enter the backstage area but the TV offers only images as the sound is drowned by songs and political speeches on stage. Around us a group of Thai journalists sit with their laptops, writing furiously. We walk down to Ratchadamri, passing again the line, long even at this time, of people getting red-shirt IDs. Along the way various tents broadcast videos of the violence on April 10. Small crowds witness images that have been repeated and repeated over and over again. We pass at least four small stalls selling CDs of the protest for fifty baht each. A long open tent on the side of the street attracts protesters with some amusement park attractions with a political undertone. With a yellow and pink backdrop the tent is divided into two sections, each with a game. In the first one, some metal bowls lie on a table, each containing three bright yellow tennis balls. Behind an old woman who distributes the balls are pyramids of cans with black and white photocopies of Abhisit's face. Twenty baht for a bucket, three throws and chances to win a cushion, quite useful in the protest. Printed on the cushions are Hello Kitty, Doraemon, or the demand for "Dissolution of Parliament," written in white on red. The latter is apparently not the most popular. In the second section a younger woman hands out darts in sets of three. A boy arranges pumped-up balloons. An old man throws. Two yellow balloons explode, exposing the face of the prime minister. Satisfied, he walks away with a Doraemon cushion.

We arrive at the barricades at the end of Ratchadamri Road. The wire mesh that appeared over the flower boxes during the day has been covered by a huge green plastic cloth, similar to what the army has used to make its units' movements invisible. Behind the wire mesh, sharpened bamboo sticks function as protection from possible invasion. It looks like a medieval barricade but for a few big truck tires, waiting to be rolled out in front of the barricade and lit with petrol in case of an army attack.

We cross to the other side and walk into Silom Road. The armed forces completely fill the streets. Thousands of them are sleeping in parking lots, hidden in buildings, and lounging in halls. Few are visible from the street but many more appear when you get into the *sois* or look into the buildings. Military hammocks hang inside elevated parking lots. We walk around into Patpong. The scene is absurd, with an uncanny resemblance to pictures of Bangkok during the Vietnam War, but all in silence and without a mass of people on the street. The place is practically empty—few stalls, almost no tourists or clients, some places are closed while in others crowds of prostitutes dressed in tight clothes or nurse outfits chitchat with young soldiers. Two guys in full military gear walk down Patpong, proudly displaying themselves, while an empty lapdance bar blasts into the street at full volume an upbeat hip-hop piece, the perfect soundtrack for their advance. They pass us as my friend's camera rolls, capturing the absurdity of the situation. We walk further down the alley. Behind some wire mesh sits a group of ten soldiers. Beside them a jeep is illuminated by the pink reflection of a neon sign for a bar, Super Pussy. We turn into a deserted Silom Road. The vision of these masses of military gives an eerie feeling to the city, accentuated by lonely prostitutes and a couple of old men dressed completely in red, walking through with smirks on their faces. We get back to Ratchadamri Road, exhausted by the heat and the walk. Here people are sleeping on the barricades, ready for something to change. About forty men with bamboo sticks wait for a full attack by thousands of heavily armed soldiers. A small group of motorcycle-taxis stands on one side. I start talking with an old man with bright white hair. He tells me in a muted tone that both sides are just "crazy with power," and that, despite what the government says, not all the motorcycle-taxis are red shirts, not even the ones that come here. Some are, but others like him come just to make money as drivers or vendors. Two younger drivers come closer and we start talking. In a few minutes clients arrive and they all leave with somebody on the rear seats. The younger one, in a purple vest, tells me to wait for him as he will be back soon.

When he gets back, a man arrives, dressed in black with a vest with "Beretta" written all over it, and calls people around. He projects self-confidence and testosterone. Soon a crowd of young men, probably the same age as the majority of the soldiers, come around to listen to him. He is explaining the situation to them and distributing, from a stuffed wallet, money for petrol to pour on the tires. "Take your motorcycle, two bikes one after the other," he instructs them. The young driver volunteers to go. He is given a hundred baht and drives away into the night.

The medieval-looking barricade at Sala Daeng intersection has been transformed and extended. An intricate puzzle of bamboo sticks now blocks the street. On April 22, a big explosion occurred in Silom Road when grenades fell from the sky, killing one person and injuring a group of citizens who were in the area to protest against the prolonged red-shirt presence. As a consequence, stakes have risen on both sides of the barricades. On the red side, the protesters have closed up the whole area behind a much higher structure covered on both sides with car and truck tires. On top of the barricade, a lonely red cartoon board in English reads, "Stop Corruption. Dissolve Parliament." In the heat of midday the asphalt underneath the barricade becomes sticky, covered in petrol that is leaking from the tires, ready to be ignited in case of an attack. From the holes in this amateur barricade, red-shirt protesters look at the other side of the street, trying to read the movements of the military. In the last few days similar structures have been erected at each entrance to the protest. Security has also been tightened. Getting in with a bike now means having to stop at the entrance while the bike compartment and your body is checked. Failure to stop can spark disproportionate reactions. A small group of people clusters underneath the Ratchadamri Skytrain station because someone has seen a soldier putting his head out of the wall of the huge racecourse stadium at the side of the street. People move around frenetically. A car and a motorcycle-taxi pass through a checkpoint without stopping. A scream sounds and some twenty very angry guys, in both red and black shirts, start running after the two vehicles. I follow them. The motorcycle-taxi is crashed onto the ground, and the driver assaulted by the men. A couple of women stop me from taking pictures and keep repeating to the guys, "There is a journalist, there is a journalist." The driver is dragged away. Small outbursts of violence occur all around the protest, effects of the palpable tension that you can sense underneath the veneer of "*rao mai klua*" (we are not scared).

The barricades now extend all the way along Rama IV Road past the entrance to Lumphini Park. I get inside through a highly patrolled entrance and park my bike. The number of people behind the bamboo wall has increased significantly. Crowds of people carrying sticks roam in the space behind a second barricade, some fifteen meters behind the big one, made of tires only. The space in between the two barricades is almost empty, just a few curious men looking at Silom through cracks in the structure. On the ground are piles of stones, their ammunition. Everybody in the city was expecting today to be the day of negotiation and maybe solution, but seen from here it really doesn't feel like it. I start asking around and protesters tell me that they expect the army to attack in the next forty-eight hours, a time limit that I have been hearing for the past week. As I stroll around having small conversations with motorcycle-taxi drivers, themselves bored by the uneventful standby, a truck with loudspeakers close to the barricades calls the *"phi nong motorcy"* (brother motorcycle-taxi drivers) to come closer and put down their names and phone numbers as they need five hundred motorcyclists to register for an unspecified mission. Immediately the people in the motorcycle-taxi group stand up and form into four half-orderly lines at a side of the truck, joined by many others, both taxi and otherwise. I join them, thinking that they will be sent out to check on the situation, talk to the police and army, and then report back. The process is complex and confused. People seem unsure of the reason they were called. Everybody is asked to write down their name, driver's license number, and phone number. Somebody suggests this is in case of damage to their bikes during patrolling so that they can be regulated and reimbursed. The process goes on for a while but nothing seems to happen and nobody moves from the area.

One after the other the drivers are registered by a group of women in their forties. As the data flows on many pieces of paper through the hands of volunteers who lean on the barricade of tires, using them as tables, the sun goes away. I decide to sit for a while, a little exhausted. I open my phone and start reading twitters. News from the stage reports the leaders' call to motorcyclists to join the protest in the following days. Apparently, during the early evening the negotiations with the government were terminated following a refusal to agree on a thirty-day dissolution deadline, effectively putting the situation back into tension and imminent confrontation. Today on stage the speeches are incendiary. News of army and police surrounding the red shirts are mixed with calls to raise the stakes and change the strategy of confrontation. Repeated calls for the protest to be nonviolent seem like a posture more than anything else, and frankly seem less and less credible. In this climate the leaders keep restating that they are ready to fight, and that they know they will win, trying to keep up the morale of the crowd. In speech after speech on stage, the motorcycle-taxi drivers are named as "motorcycle heroes." Nattawut Saikua gets on stage and starts enumerating the weaponry, policemen, and soldiers deployed by the state. He follows this with the red shirts' defenses. "We have six lines of defense already. Two thousand motorcycle volunteers are needed at each entrance," he says. This is probably the reason why the names were collected at the barricades. One after the other, the leaders of the movement step on stage, talking about the ongoing confrontation, always leaving with some words about the "motorcycle heroes."

At Ratchaprasong the crowd has grown significantly since the last time I was here. As I move away from the stage I hear from the loudspeakers the word "motorcycle-taxi." I turn around and on stage is a motorcycle-taxi driver, dressed in a vest with the insignia of the Phuea Thai Party. He talks to the crowd about the two hundred thousand motorcycle-taxis in this city who support the movement because Thaksin gave them freedom from local mafia. "We will come out to help the red shirts," he assures as the crowd claps. He speaks very briefly. Dr. Weng Tojirakarn, a longtime leader of the democracy movement, is again on stage thanking him. I start running toward the stage, trying to meet this guy. I manage to get backstage. Nobody seems to have seen him. I ask Sean Bungprakorn, the international spokesman of the red shirts, and Jaran Dittha-apichai, one of the leaders. Both seem to have no idea. They both sit on plastic chairs in front of two TVs whose sound is impossible to hear because both their phones ring endlessly. When I ask Jaran how I can contact him he tells me that it is not a good time. Both he and Sean don't seem to think they are going to be attacked today but they seem sure they will be eventually. "On

Monday morning," Jaran says with certainty, "astrologers said that the twenty-sixth is going to be a very bad day for Thailand." His phone rings and he walks away to let a journalist in. I roam away to look backstage where the leaders and some monks are chatting with well-dressed, good-looking young ladies who seem out of a fashion magazine rather than at a "peasant" protest.

Back at the table, Jaran invites me to eat with him. He says that they will have elections and then reintroduce the 1997 constitution. I push him a bit. "Your answers have to do with the immediate changes but don't deal with the more structural problems and issues that the red shirts are talking about such as inequality and double standards." He tells me that it is a long process and they need to get rid of the aristocracy first. I tell him that aristocracy in the end takes its power from one source and it is difficult to think of one without the other. A younger guy close to him smiles, staring at Jaran to read an answer on his face. Jaran lowers his head and voice. "I don't know what the future will look like but definitely we need something different from this," pointing to the crowd at the other side of the stage. I then ask him about the military intervention and the risk of protesters dying. "Soldiers too," he says. "They may even win here in Ratchaprasong but not in the nation," he adds with cold eyes. "If they attack, the whole area will be destroyed, the buildings, everything." He keeps repeating, "It will be civil war" and "We will win big." Scary words to hear from a man like this. I leave shortly afterwards and ride back, stopping to take pictures of the lines of people still registering for the red-shirt ID card and a crowd watching a mega screen where Jatuporn Prompan speaks about the situation. He opens every sentence with, "I learned from *phi nong* here," and concludes saying that if they are attacked it will be Rwanda two. I pass again through the small opening in the barricades and drive back home through the silent city. Tomorrow is going to be motorcycle day.

THE NATION

GOVT WARNS OF TOUGH ACTION

» PM: Will not allow demonstrators to leave Rajprasong site and cause confusion in city

» Suthep: Any protesters setting up illegal checkpoints, causing unrest will be arrested

Newin vows to protect the monarchy

Seven permanent checkpoints manned by a joint force of police and soldiers have been set up around the red shirts' protest site at Rajprasong.

International tourist arrivals plunge drastically in wake of political turmoil

The average number of arrivals is now about **20,000 a day,** down from 30,000 prior to the start of protests at the Phan Fa Bridge on March 14, Tourism and Sports Minister Chumpol said yesterday.

For the first time I arrive at the protest early in the morning. The tension of yesterday and the sleepless wait for an attack, which every night seems imminent but never occurs, has left people tired, sleeping anywhere they can find a place. It is rare to see Thai people sleeping so late, especially people from the countryside and service workers, who usually are the first to wake up and open the windows and shops of the city. The protest site is at its emptiest. Like every morning, many people have gone to their jobs, leaving the square to a few people listening to some low-level speakers and small groups lounging in the shade. I get in from Rama IV Road with the intention of following the motorcyclists' actions today. The barricades are surprisingly empty, some people sleeping and the smell of breakfast soup being cooked and steaming sticky rice being readied in bamboo canisters to feed people for the coming day. I talk briefly to a guy dressed in black about what is going on and he tells me that the bikes went out earlier to collect information on the troops' movements. A truck with loudspeakers and a large board showing pictures of the tenth stands still and silent in the morning heat. At its side is a pile of boxes filled with helmets, which have been brought to distribute to the "heroes" of the red shirts. I remount my bike and easily ride through Ratchadamri, silent and rather empty, disturbed only by the noises of people waking up and the smell of food. A lonely speaker broadcasts without the usual response from people or the roar of a crowd.

I ride towards Siam Square hoping to find a different scene with the presence of motorcycles but I pass through scene after scene with the same atmosphere of a village waking up, right in the middle of ultra-modern Bangkok. I stop at the intersection between Henry Dunant and Rama I Roads, where normally a cobbler sits. A small group of drivers is gathered under the shadow of a stall with a hammock attached. The whole stall vibrates with the oscillating body of a chubby driver lounging in the hammock. Most of the drivers are from this district and they have been coming every morning to make money and support the red shirts. We start talking about politics, ideas about the red shirts, and the role of motorcycle-taxis. It is the usual talk about Thaksin and his attempt to free the drivers from "influential people," even if one of them keeps repeating that mafia are still present in their lives. We talk for a while, mostly with an old man who seems to be the most vocal in the group. His vest, worn over a red T-shirt, shows that he normally works close by. I ask him what the motorcycle-taxis are supposed to do that day and he tells me that they have already gone to the prime minister's house, following rumors that he was there, but found the house empty. As we talk about motorcycle-taxis he keeps repeating that speed is the key element, their speed in action, appearing and disappearing. As some of them ride away and come back in the course of work, I get into a conversation with others about social welfare states and taxi systems. As usual I'm struck by their knowledge and curiosity. At some point I am left with the only woman in the group. She is forty-two and has two kids. Her vest says Dusit but she normally works somewhere else on the outskirts of the city. She is not a particular supporter of the red shirts but comes here to earn money for her kids and leaves every afternoon to go back to her family, getting more money than she normally would. She smiles with shyness, her long bleached hair flowing on her shoulders. The day passes dully, taken hostage by the pressing feeling of an imminent violent turn.

The sun comes up on an almost silent central business district. On one side of the barricades a few soldiers stay awake, while their comrades sleep hidden in spaces between buildings, in parking lots, or inside empty apartments. Some soldiers come out of an underground parking lot in Sala Daeng Soi 1 in an orderly fashion and take up position under the Skytrain. A few people walk down Silom, emptied of office workers and vendors. On the other side of the barricades, the protest takes its first morning steps. Slowly, crowds of people stand up from their mats and quietly walk to a bus transformed into public bathrooms or to handmade cubicles where people take a shower behind a blue plastic sheet. Where normally the only smell is the smog of traffic, a pungent aroma of steaming sticky rice fills the air. Some younger protesters, relieved by the sun, hurry to their village tent, ready to hit the mattress after a long vigilant night. Another day starts its course in the protest, tense but calm.

Some hours later, motorcycles start converging at the corner of Ratchadamri Road and Sarasin Road, at first, just a few dozen, dressed in bright orange motorcycle-taxi vests, led by a middle-aged man sitting on a bike sporting a two-meter-high Thai flag. He looks around from behind aviator sunglasses, his face covered by a white surgical mask. His vest bears the logo of Phuea Thai Party. On its back are three messages: "We love the King," "Nonviolence," and "We are Thai. We think differently but we are not divided." As the minutes go by, more motorcyclists join the group, form into lines, and move slowly towards the intersection with Witthayu Road. Here the procession, now composed of about five hundred bikes, often carrying two passengers, stops for a long while to prepare and discuss the direction. Some motorcycle-taxi drivers, following the direction of the middle-aged man, start collecting the names and license plates of the drivers, "in case somebody gets arrested." I see the orange vests disappear, carefully folded away. Drivers cover their license plates with boards or plastic bags. "This way they will not know who is who," one tells me. On my left a monk lights a cigarette, puffing smoke around him. After about an hour the procession finally starts moving, compact, through the city. I get on my bike and follow them.

The heat is merciless. The procession keeps halting to remain in lockstep, moving in the direction of Din Daeng. The bikes cross the central business district and passersby look rather confused, often meeting the moving convoy with scared gazes and perplexed eyes. A few people on the street cheer the protesters, offer drinks, or greet members of the moving convoy. The situation changes suddenly as soon as the procession passes an invisible line that divides the commercial area from the lower-income apartments in Din Daeng Road. From here on, hordes of people lining the streets cheer, greet, offer support, or just salute. The convoy grows at every corner as new bikes and pickups join in. "Red areas" and "yellow areas" are becoming a new way of organizing space in the city, determining levels of comfort or danger, depending on your affiliation. "Sure they bring food to the military in Silom," somebody told me yesterday. "It is a yellow area, but let's see what will happen in Lat Phrao. Military there have to be careful about how they move when they enter red areas." These days, all around the city, wrist bands and small flags are taken off or put on depending on the area, as a new geography, often overlapping with the geography of inequality, is reshaping dwellers' perceptions of their city, creating new borders like the one we just passed.

Supported by more and more people coming out of their houses and offices, the convoy cruises into Vibhavadi Rangsit Road. Small trucks with loudspeakers call on people to join the procession, now going towards a big fresh market on the outskirts of the city. Usual traffic flows smoothly, embraced by a sea of red bikes. Just beyond Don Muang Airport, the traffic suddenly comes to a halt, and the red convoy stops. A few bikes zigzag through the cars to see what is going on in front. Nervousness shakes the crowd as rumors start circulating of an imminent army attack. Bikes are sent off by the leaders to check possible exit routes from the jam. A few minutes later the bikes come back with bad news. Every exit seems closed by groups of soldiers, lined up behind anti-riot shields. I drive to the front to take a look. As soon as I park the bike, a few tear gas shots break the standstill, followed by rounds of rubber bullets. It is craziness again.

People run away to hide from bullets bouncing off the concrete overpasses before hitting the ground. Confusion reigns for some minutes as the soldiers advance, covered by shots coming from the highway over us, where other soldiers have taken up position. I run into a small *soi* and take refuge inside a building. Locals tell us that there is no exit from this *soi*, urging everyone to move away before the army advances. I pick up an old woman and ride back, dodging rubber bullets. The group reconvenes a few hundred meters back. People start moving traffic signs and tree branches to the middle of the street to create small barricades. In a few minutes people appear with sharpened bamboo sticks and iron bars. A man passes me carrying a table leg. Hell breaks loose again as the air gets itchy, filled by tear gas. Some groups of protesters hide behind the barricades, pushing them toward the military. Others behind scream warnings for them not to get closer. A monk with a bamboo stick walks around, eyes red. The first injured are carried back from the front lines. The more peaceful protesters look around in fear and confusion, trying to find a way out. As the tension grows, a providential heavy rain hits the battleground, cooling the spirits. From behind the protesters, lines of police officers in anti-riot gear appear, now completely surrounding the group and thousands of local dwellers who have joined them in the street. Torrential rain soaks protesters and government forces alike. We remain there for almost an hour, trying to figure out what happens next. The police lines start advancing. A few protesters start negotiating with them. I get closer. The police officer in charge is talking to a protester who carries a walkie-talkie with a long antenna. "We are here to protect you," the officer says calmly. "We are not going to attack you." The protester goes back and tries to calm down his side, fearing that someone might do something stupid.

As negotiation goes on, overseen by the soldiers on the highway, more and more police trucks arrive in the area. Suddenly hordes of police officers in normal uniform, without weapons or protection, come out of the vans and pass the anti-riot police, cheered by the locals and the protesters. For some time the two sides engage in a strange dance, advancing and retreating as if in a collective courting ritual. After about twenty minutes, the police officers in uniform tell the protesters to move to one side and pass them. The police take up position between the army and the red shirts. Once a long line is formed, the police, with their backs to the soldiers, effectively shield the protesters who finally have an exit route. The crowd in the street cheers and applauds the police officers as the procession slowly moves into the flooded back streets, making its way back to the Ratchaprasong area, always headed by a small vanguard checking the street and directing the convoy. For the second time in a few weeks, the police mediated between the protesters and the army, diffusing tension. A new player seems to have entered the chessboard, with an unclear role.

The violence that broke out during the procession towards Don Muang was far away from the protest area, yet the tense standstill has built up a palpable sense that a violent turn is approaching. Day after day, rumors have spread of army movements and of suspicious maneuvers on top of high-rise buildings in the area, making people peer upwards with a mixture of fear and excitement. The barricades on the Silom side have been repeatedly moved during the last few days, taken down and then rapidly reconstructed during the night, leaving access to the Chulalongkorn Hospital free and creating a porous border to the protest. Now in front of Chulalongkorn Hospital, which was clumsily raided by a group of red shirts who were looking for soldiers but instead only succeeded in scaring patients, a long wall of bamboo sticks and tires runs along the road divider on Ratchadamri up to the end of Lumphini Park. The large space in front of Lumphini Park is a detached island from the protest, connected by a thin and claustrophobic corridor that runs all the way up to the Skytrain station and then across the street, reducing the area of the protest but also balancing the visual effect of the diminishing number of people. The other side of the corridor, facing the hospital, teems with police officers with small cameras or cell phones, calmly taking pictures of their colleagues standing in front of the barricades. Again, as during the clash with the convoy, the presence of the police works as a sedative on the red shirts.

Officers dressed in anti-riot gear look curiously through the holes in the handmade barricade, mirrored by protesters on the other side. It is not long before the two groups start talking to each other, joking about each others' looks. Often the conversations slip from Thai into Isan dialect, marking the shared regional identity of some of the protesters and the policemen. Across an intricate bundle of bamboo, rubber, and wire mesh, conversations sparkle. Behind the barricades, piles of stones rise from the ground, ready to be thrown. Soon a small crowd of foreign journalists gathers, puzzled by this moment. As cameras start shooting, high-ranking officers sitting in the shade call the police officers away from the barricade. Some bottles of water are passed though the holes before the groups are called back to their ranks.

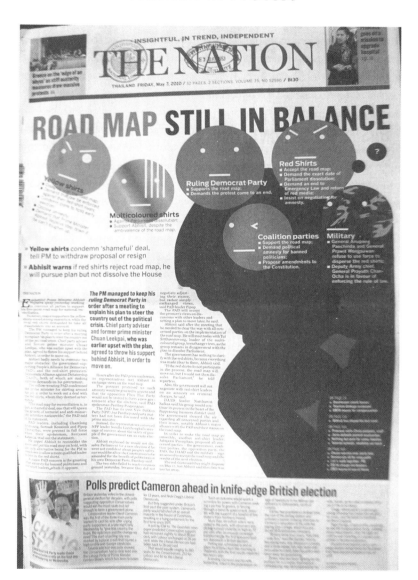

Day after day, as discourses, threats, rumors, and promises go almost un-listened to and scenes of people cooking sticky rice protected by the shadow of a multi-million-baht shopping mall becomes normality, life at the protest goes on as usual. New groups of people from Isan keep arriving to replenish the outflow of the last few days, making the area a bit more crowded than of late. More than a month has gone by and there seems to be no visible sign of resolution. The government will probably not allow the protesters to obtain a dissolution of parliament, scared of the precedent that would be set, and the red shirts will not lose face and just leave. This realization has been spreading lately, reviving the negotiation between the two sides. Backstage has also been transformed to accommodate this new phase. Chairs have been moved to create a small conference area, with a large table covered by white cloth over a backdrop with black and white pictures of the people who died on the tenth and a huge banner saying "Dissolution" topped by "So that our friends didn't die for nothing." In the last few days many of the speeches, especially the more media-oriented, have been delivered by the whole group of leaders and broadcast from here, instead of from the stage, changing the incendiary rhetoric and posture on stage to a more "civilized" and calm arrangement, with the leaders talking calmly at a table. In a time of resuscitated negotiation, sitting at a table becomes a physical and metaphorical strategy. In this new space, leaders and their guards sit chatting on small plastic chairs underneath the stage before stepping up. The international spokesman is sitting in front of cameras with no operator behind them. When he finishes he proudly shows the system of broadcasting by which any event can be posted in real time on the UDD's Facebook page, to bypass state censorship of the red TV and radio channels. As usual, the spokesman makes introductions and then walks away. A few minutes after, I find myself working as a translator for a Spanish documentary filmmaker who is exploring the role of women's activism in the red-shirt movement.

We jump over a metal fence that divides the stage area from the crowd, mostly composed of women, and sit there for a while interviewing three middle-aged women, who crowd around the camera, taking turns under the spotlight, shouting to overcome the noise coming from the stage. All of them are currently living in Bangkok, even if born outside the city. One of them is the wife of a doctor who, she says, supports the cause but does not have time to come to Ratchaprasong. "The involvement of women in the red shirts," she says, surrounded by a sea of ladies, "is first an answer to a practical problem. As our husbands have a fixed job they have no time to come here, so we come to support the red shirts on behalf of all of our families." She looks at the other two women. They agree with a nod and giggle. One of them says, "As women we know what the problems are. We see our kids' daily life, the house, the education. As our husbands go to work and come back home to drink, we see every day the inequality of this country." As we discuss, more people around get into the conversation, if just for a moment. Fruit, water, and booklets are constantly distributed from the lower stage to the people in front. Pieces of paper circulate as everybody writes her name and phone number. A middle-aged ladyboy working in an office joins the group. Behind us a woman sits on a small chair with a huge hat shaped like Democracy Monument. The conversation is continuously interrupted by loud noises from the stage. The crowd grows as the sun goes down, ready for another evening of political discussions and songs. I appreciate their resilience but I do not think I can stand another night of the same discourses.

A mixture of tension, fear, excitement, and boredom has been conquering the protesters over the past few days. Day after day, predictable discourses and sleepless nights set the rhythm of the protest and the daily lives of many who participate alongside their normal schedules. At sunrise many leave the protest only to return in the evening. Behind these fluctuations and daily diasporas stand a multitude of stories, lives, and motivations. Regional migrants leave the protest in the morning to service the city that is slowly eating their lives. Some go back to their hometowns to visit relatives, taking advantage of the free buses connecting the city and the villages. Small businesses take advantage of the protesters' presence in the city to support their families, beyond any issue of political convictions. Curiosity about the wonders of the metropolis takes protesters out of the protest area at times. Some come back because of political ideals, democracy, equality; some come back to get a free bowl of food; some want for once to be part of history, to touch it, to make it; some seize the chance to take the girl from the shop next door to somewhere different on a date; some others "go home," as they put it, to experience the nostalgia of their lives in the village, either by truly going to their village, or just to its encampment in the middle of the bustling metropolis.

Every night, after a long day's work, on the streets or sitting on his old bike waiting for clients, my friend Adun stretches his back, takes off his vest, and goes "home" to see friends from his village, eat with them, and sit in the village tent, chain-smoking cigarettes, with political speeches in the background that he barely cares about. "I have heard them before," he tells me, smiling. "They always say the same thing. I agree with them but I'd rather talk to people from home, hear news of what is going on back there, and have nice food. I am here anyway and I am ready to help if something happens." Many like Adun have supported the red shirts for a long time in the private space of their homes and minds, but never went to protests before. Now the gravitational force of acquaintances brings them here. After all, political participation is not taking place in the world of old German philosophers, who starve their own family to death while they receive money from a rich friend to write ideological pamphlets, but in the world of people who struggle every day just to make ends meet, who work and save money to send back to their families, to send their children to a decent school, and to have some extra money at the end of the week to drink with friends, bet on sports, or waste it on something else. It is these people's silent torments, daily struggles, growing dissatisfactions that, when vocalized, create political movements and have a chance at changing history. At times, all that is needed for taking this step is a friend they haven't seen for a while, a distant aunt who is sleeping at the protest, the longing for a homemade papaya salad from their village. Tonight Adun called me to suggest, "Come with me to my home."

Adun, three other motorcycle-taxi drivers, and I enter the protest area on bikes. None of them are wearing their vests. "It is too dangerous," they tell me. We ride through the protest, enjoying the feeling of being in a small convoy, getting close to each other to talk as we ride. On the wall at the northern side of Lumphini Park a painted stencil says "Red Land." We park and walk back to the stall from Bangdung, Adun's district in Udon Province. At one corner of the tent, a small crowd is gathered around a large TV screen showing still pictures of bullets and bullet wounds. A man in his fifties, well-dressed and with a charming look, talks into a microphone, describing each bullet type, its range and deadly potential, and showing pictures of the damage that it can cause. Like a vocal vendor at a village fair, he senses the feelings of the crowd with great empathy and alternates information and pictures, passing around real bullets, sealed in two hermetic plastic bags. At the stall in front, a small projector shows images from April 10, but with no sound. Warfare education. Where I saw this before, things ended up turning ugly.

We sit down with some people in the stall. Immediately, food with hot sticky rice is brought to us. A man from the village who worked in Phuket for many years talks to me in a mixture of English and Italian. Cosmopolitan villagers, one would say. Adun goes around greeting people, leaving me to my conversation. Beside us sits a group of men in their forties whom I have never seen before at the tent. A small older crowd sits a few meters away. A young man dressed in black speaks about the imminent violence. "We are ready to fight," he tells all of us with serious eyes "We are organized and we have no fear of dying." As he says this, another guy of the same age arrives with some cans of beer hidden in small plastic bags. "Drink," he tells me, "but keep it in the bag. The guards don't want us to get drunk." Adun looks at him with a mixture of respect and derision. "I have known him since he was a kid," he tells me with half a smile. I leave them and walk away to sit with the older crowd. I have seen two of the women before, but the older men look unfamiliar. I ask. "We just arrived yesterday," they say sitting cross-legged and shouting over the noise from the speakers on stage. "Somebody came around to the village and told us that they needed people at the protest and our tent was getting emptier. So we decided to come to Bangkok. They organized a car from the village and brought us here." "Did you also get some money?" I ask. "No, no money but we had a free ride and here we don't have to pay for food or sleeping." "I have been back and forth three times already," an older woman in a sarong tells me. "The first time at Phan Fa Bridge and the other two here. I stay for some time and then go back when I miss home or I get bored. There is not much to do here."

A constant refill of people is organized from the countryside, where the grassroots movement has permeated the territory. A phone call comes from someone at the protest, or some organizer spreads the word that new people are needed in Bangkok. Volunteers step forward and the crowd is kept constant at the protest. "We came on behalf of the many others who cannot, who have a job, or have to look after children. We are old so we can come but we are here for our children and nephews too." She points out an older woman to me. I ask, "Is this your first time in Bangkok?" "No, I have been here before. My daughter works here, but I don't like the city. I came to support the red shirts." I turn to the larger group. "So do you like being here?" A moment of silence. "It's boring," a woman breaks the silence and they all laugh with embarrassment. Behind them Veera Musikapong, one of the leaders, is on screen, his words resounding from lines of loudspeakers down Ratchadamri Road.

Two men in the group look up for a second. "Look at this. He's a good speaker but also boring. He sounds like a monk. When Nattawut (Saikua) is on stage it is more fun." I go back to the other group of people and chat for a while, sitting on mats, as slowly the stalls fall quiet, with sleeping bodies filling the space. Adun hits the mat and I say goodbye to him and ride back home, passing small groups of sleepy people still carrying bamboo sticks behind the barricade facing Silom Road.

t has started. For some days now it has seemed evident that the negotiations were not going to lead to any real solution, but today a high-speed bullet tore apart the facade of expectation and uncertainty. This bullet, shot just after sunset by unknown yet guessable hands, pierced the head of Seh Daeng, the military "hero" of the red shirts, leaving him in a puddle of blood on the pavement during an interview with a *New York Times* reporter. Rumors run around the city about his health but it seems obvious that his body will not survive for long without a functioning brain. It did not take too long for the red shirts to understand that this was going to be the beginning of the army's movements. Hordes of protesters start pouring onto the streets around the protest area where occasional shootings are taking place, echoing through otherwise empty roads. Around 11:00 p.m. I decide to take a look, taking advantage of a slowdown in the shooting and fighting. The Silom area looks deserted. Few shops are open. The army has blocked the streets with orange plastic barriers, securing their own exit in case of more protesters arriving. Most of the fighting is occurring at the end of Silom and Witthayu Roads. I put on a green Press band and walk through the street. The tension is palpable. Almost nobody is on the streets besides military and security personnel. A small crowd of people with small pins of the Thai flag, "no-color people" as they call themselves, sit on the stairs of a 7-Eleven, still open, at the corner of Convent Road. We talk briefly. One of them carries a stick and keeps talking about fighting, protected by the soldiers. After a few minutes, a long round of shooting fills the air, coming from Sala Daeng. The small crowd disperses as the 7-Eleven closes down. In the middle of craziness sometimes small details hit you. The reality of this moment slaps me as the metal shutter hits the ground. I have never in my life seen a 7-Eleven close. In Thailand, the chain's ubiquitous 24/7 service screams at you from every corner. Normality is gone, I think, as I ride in the direction of Rama IV Road.

Underneath an elevated bridge a big crowd of red shirts gather. Men, women, and students roam around disoriented as a few taxis and a mass of motorcycles fill the streets about a kilometer away from the two conflict areas. At the corner in front of the Lumphini Night Market, five or six ambulances are parked, ready to go. The atmosphere is extremely tense. In the dark area lit by few lights, the mass of people moves frenetically without direction. Some people shout, others run towards Sala Daeng to throw stones. Occasionally, shots reverberate in the area and everybody tries to hide under the bridge. The more active groups, mostly composed of younger men, visibly drunk and high, talk among themselves with the attitude of youngsters looking for a boost to their adrenaline rather than the trained guerrilla fighters that the government is depicting. A man in his forties, dressed in large jeans and a white T-shirt that covers a well-shaped body, shouts at the top of his lungs that the army is killing people and everybody here has a wife and children yet everybody is there because of their love of democracy and of Thailand. People clap. He starts every sentence with "I am not a leader but…" A younger man wearing a blue Chelsea Football Club T-shirt, almost in a trance, shouts "I am red in the heart," with his hands first spread to the sky and then clasped back over his chest. Adrenaline makes people do strange things; alcohol and amphetamines probably help too. Suddenly all the ambulances are in motion, bringing injured protesters from the Witthayu area. I get close to a patient. He doesn't seem to be shot. Yet everybody is moving as if he is really sick. A rumor, passed around by word of mouth and later confirmed, claims that a man with a Channel 3 journalist badge showed up at a corner fifty meters away with coffee and water that was distributed to protesters in 7-Eleven cups. Many people drank them and soon started feeling dizzy. Ambulances pass by at speed, driving about twenty of these people to a nearby hospital. A young man in the black apparel worn by the movement's guards and a bulletproof vest stands on top of his motorcycle, trying to collect people on motorcycle to go up the road, help the people affected, and look for the mysterious guy who brought the coffee. A small crowd forms around him but nobody seems to jump on their bikes. Then a woman stands on her bike and immediately people start moving.

The atmosphere in the direction of Sarasin Road is strangely calm. There are few people, and the government has cut off the lighting, effectively creating a sort of empty buffer zone for the conflict. In the complete darkness, a few lights move, covered by cloth to be less visible to the soldiers, who are reported to be inside Lumphini Park. I walk in the dark, accompanied by a small group of drunken youths. I can feel people walking in silence around me, shadows moving in between buildings, fleeting shapes. The sense of time changes in these situations of tension. Minutes seem to drag on endlessly until breath is interrupted by the sound of a shot that echoes in the hot night. In the dark I meet a Thai videographer friend. He just arrived from a conflict zone and he is still shaken by the vision of a man shot in the neck. He sits in the dark, alone. It is almost funny how you can judge the danger level of a spot by the presence or absence of video and photo journalists. If an area is full of them, move away. It is dangerous. If an area has none of them, it is safe. You can stay. I leave him sitting and get closer to the end of Sarasin Road. Turning a corner, I am back into the usual protest scene. Generators provide light. A group of people sing under a tent as others sleep quietly, as if they were hours away from the conflict.

The situation is increasingly tense and surreal, the city is transformed into a war zone, at least in its core—Silom, Sathorn, Rama IV, Pratunam, and Din Daeng. Razor wire in the middle of the street blocks people from joining the protest or bringing supplies to the red area. Lines of soldiers stand in the sun. Rounds of shots fill the emptied spaces between buildings. Small crowds of protesters gather here and there, hiding behind buildings or bridges, eyes to the air trying to spot snipers. Sathorn Road, one of the main arteries of the central business district, is eerie in its emptiness. The usually buzzing road has been transformed into a buffer space filled with the anticipation of more violence, a looming crackdown. In the small crowds of red shirts the mantra is that the population is not "accepting" the actions of the army and government. Rumors spread of people being killed and disappearing. In front of the Australian Embassy, military in full gear stand in the heat, facing a small crowd of people and motorcycles that is growing at the entrance of Suan Phlu, hooting their horns and shouting to the soldiers from afar. The military side is even tenser. A line of soldiers prevents people from taking pictures or videos. Smaller detachments move furtively, hiding behind the road divider, with their weapons pointed at whatever moves close to them. Behind them, heavy fighting is going on at the Rama IV intersection, the center of confrontation now. Loud explosions are heard from the direction of Silom, grenades detonating and echoing in empty streets surrounded by inert buildings. In the eyes of these soldiers all you read is growing fear as the fighting flares behind them. As I try in vain to convince the soldiers to let me through the roadblock, two French men in short pants and colorful T-shirts walk along the sidewalk, pull out a map, and ask me how to get to Siam Square. I look around confused. The soldier I am talking to stares at the two tourists in disbelief and tells them to walk away.

I walk them back, trying to explain to the two men why it is not a very good idea to go shopping in Siam Square now. More people pour onto the street at the entrance of Suan Phlu, driven by the spreading news of military action. For now, people just stand on their motorcycles in the middle of the street, carefully watching every movement of the soldiers, ready to react or just take cover somewhere. This is the perfect recipe for a really nasty ending.

Down the road, Soi Atthakanprasit (Soi 1) is completely closed to traffic. One motorcycle-taxi driver comes around telling everybody to be careful in the back *sois* as some soldiers are reported to be shooting rubber bullets at motorcyclists between Ngam Duphli and Rama IV Roads. An older driver, sitting inside Suan Phlu on his bike, half looking at the situation and half picking up clients who go in the direction of Narathiwat, tells me they are going to set buildings on fire all over the city tonight. This is a nightmare for the soldiers, now surrounded by small but growing crowds of mostly local young men. More news arrives, again carried by motorcycle-taxi drivers, that another group of red shirts is gathering at the Khlong Toei slum, ready to attack the army. A pattern is forming, concentric circles alternating between red shirts and army, decreasing in density away from the center. As I write this, a round of gunshots arrives from the entrance of Suan Phlu. I decide it is a good time to get back home.

As the sun goes down, my apartment in the middle of the conflict area resounds with continuous rounds of firing. At some point during the day, their sound changed. "The rubber bullets are finished," says a friend over the phone. On TV, the government spokesman repeats that the soldiers are using live rounds to defend themselves. Adun arrived at my house in the late afternoon and asked me if he could stay here in order to be close to the protest areas if something happens. His wife had been asking him to go back to Bangdung so he is going to leave tomorrow to catch a local fireworks festival there. He is visibly tormented, alternating between wanting to go to the conflict area and help his friends and a feeling of impotence at this situation. He keeps repeating that this could not happen in the countryside where people have weapons in their houses. He is trying to stay calm as his phone rings continuously, mostly from people in his district tent in the core of the protest, who can hear shots but have no idea of what is going on around them. Adun tells me that the red shirts themselves have unplugged most of the lights there, leaving much of the area in the dark. In the protest, now impossible to reach from outside, remain mostly old people and women listening to the leaders' speeches that report only parts of the news in order to keep the morale high. Not only flows of people and goods but also flows of information are being blocked or redirected around the area. Two of the three major phone services are unstable. The national news for the most part reports sporadically and one-sidedly on the protests, while the popular Spring News TV, which has been earning a reputation for fair reporting, has been blocked today by the government propaganda apparatus.

Adun and I sit on my couch, watching Thai boxing and trying to filter news that arrives by phone, from CNN and BBC, and by twitters that I translate to him. We watch videos from the internet about the protest and have a long discussion on how international media are doing a better job than locals at, as he says, "having a more complete picture." "Thai people abroad know better than us what is going on," he concludes. In the late afternoon, dotted now by sporadic sounds of explosions and rifle rounds, Adun is no longer able to keep watching these images. He sits in front of the window, listening on his cell phone to the radio broadcast from the red-shirt stage. He stands up every time a long round of shots resounds, trying to locate their origin, screening with his eyes the familiar geography of Sathorn.

We go out again around 11:00 p.m. The crowd of red-shirt supporters in Soi Suan Phlu is still growing. About sixty bikes are parked at the corner of Suan Phlu and many other people have gathered there out of curiosity or support for the red cause. Public lighting has been cut off all along Sathorn up to the Narathiwat intersection. The cars and bikes coming out of Suan Phlu are advised by some red-shirt supporters carrying walkie-talkies to put out their lights for their own security. The atmosphere is gloomy, lit by red flames and black smoke coming from tires burning in the middle of the street in front of the Shell petrol station. The motorcycle-taxi drivers are now directing the traffic out of Suan Phlu. A few *farang* living in the area walk around. The soldiers, still located near the Australian Embassy, are occasionally shooting in this direction but over our heads. Every round is met with a loud cheer from the crowd. Down Suan Phlu the echoes of the shooting make an uncommon background for the apparently normal daily life of the locals eating at street vendors. At the front of Suan Phlu some young protesters shout to others to change their shirts and dress in black. A middle-aged man shoots fireworks at the army. Today protesters took off their red shirts, making themselves very difficult for the military to identify. A young taxi driver is listening with a small red transmitter to the hospital radio, feeding people information about the injured and the ongoing fighting. This is going to be a long night, even in a peripheral area of the confrontation.

A couple of hours later, a friend from Isan decides to pass by the house. I find him and his friends outside my door, completely drunk on their motorcycles. The friends included two motorcycle-taxi drivers and an office worker who keeps talking to me in some sort of English that nobody else would understand. She keeps repeating in her loud drunken voice that we should all go to support the "red army." The others keep asking her why and telling her no. We sit upstairs on the rooftop and talk about the situation, weapons, sniper rifles and their techniques, blathering about things we know nothing about. The conversation flows from one subject to the other, interrupted by the craziness of this situation. The talk and the alcohol put all of us into a strange mood. "Seeing these images, living this situation makes me sick. I want to do something to support my brothers but I don't know what I can do," says one of them, bringing on a moment of silence. The conversation is occasionally punctuated by an abrupt round of shots. The woman immediately falls silent, puts her hands together, and starts praying in a soft and monotonous tone, while the three men stand up and try to locate the direction of the shots and I look up my phone for twitter updates. We are a strange group, sitting above the city in a silence broken occasionally by the woman's prayers and the disapproving clicks of our mouths.

In the morning Suan Phlu is restored to normality and the small crowd at the beginning of the *soi* is gone. Soi Atthakanprasit remains closed behind Q-House where about twenty soldiers rest in the shade cast by the walls around the building. Soi Ngam Duphli, however, is completely transformed by the ongoing fighting. The *soi* is relatively empty and the motorcycle-taxis, normally standing at every corner, are gone. It's not clear where. As I get closer to the Rama IV intersection, a small crowd of about fifty people sits on their motorcycles and on the ground in front of a burning rubbish bin. Rama IV Road looks like a postwar zone. Smoke rises from a garbage collection truck in the middle of the street in front of the side entrance to Suan Lum Night Bazaar. Behind the truck the army has built a small wall of black sandbags. A tense silence fills the huge empty road covered in debris, burning tires, and broken glass from small hand-made Molotov cocktails and shattered phone booths. From time to time, a man walks out of the small crowd and shouts, amplified by an orange traffic cone, "Buffaloes!" or "Animals!" at the army. The soldiers reply with a short round of rubber bullets in the air. The silence is restored by the soft sounds of rubber bullets falling on the ground. On the other side of Rama IV Road towards Khlong Toei, four big truck tires are burning, filling the air with thick black smoke. Inside Soi Ngam Duphli, back from the crowd, a small group of men drinking beer show me the signs of bullets on the walls around the area.

As I talk to them, a young man in black gear walks past me carrying a plastic bag filled with small empty Red Bull bottles. A piece of cloth emerges from a hole pierced in the cap of each bottle. The guy sits on the sidewalk at the entrance of the *soi* and starts filling the bottles with petrol. The scene is grotesque. He throws a mini-Molotov to smash on the ground but it produces no fire. The crowd voices its disappointment and laughs. The guy keeps making more, trying to find a working mixture. He and his friends seem anything but highly trained paramilitary forces. In the middle of this, an old Australian walks slowly across Rama IV Road trying to take pictures with his small cell phone. He walks up and asks me if I know how to take pictures on the phone. After I show him he walks back happily, ignoring my call to be careful. Some people hide behind smashed phone booths, firing small stones at the soldiers with slingshots.

Silom Road has been closed by the military, checking who goes in and out. Down Surawong Road, the street has been closed but it is possible to pass through the block with a motorbike going in the direction of MBK department store. This whole section of Rama IV Road is completely empty, dotted with orange plastic barriers, razor wire, and small groups of soldiers sitting in the shadows. The place is surreal in comparison to a normal day but the atmosphere is relatively relaxed. I ride down the empty Rama IV Road past Wat Hualamphong. Monks walk past three green chairs where military men sit in full gear, their guns leaning against the base of a tree. Three motorcycle-taxi drivers are waiting for clients that I doubt will ever arrive. At the intersection with Ratchathewi, orange barriers and razor wire block the street completely. I am not sure if some tear gas was fired here earlier but the air itches. I ride back. Sathorn Road is also completely closed to traffic, but here the police patrol the area. This is the frontier of the conflict. Outside that area there is an uncanny emptiness and a few patrols driving around.

I decide to go back to Soi Ngam Duphli. The narrow *soi* now ends in a thick wall of black smoke that completely fills the small space between the buildings on Rama IV Road. The crowd is much bigger than in the morning. Tires have been piled up. Molotovs have also gone "pro": larger bottles and a higher success rate. Tires are constantly rolled into Rama IV and lit with a small battery of Molotovs, to cover the view towards the other red barricade, situated three hundred meters down Rama IV in the direction of Khlong Toei. Everybody is wearing a white mask, distributed by a guy on a motorcycle down the *soi*. Everybody moves carefully, keeping close to the left walls of the *soi*, as they say two people have been shot dead and a paramedic injured as they were standing in the middle of the street. Three bullet holes in a window on the right side of the street seem to confirm gunshots coming from a building above us. Down the *soi*, three trucks of firefighters wait to see how the situation evolves. At the corner with Rama IV, about twenty people squat behind a wall of tires, stored for future burning. Some of them throw Molotovs to keep the tires burning and shoot loose stones from slingshots in the direction of the army. I have not seen any other weapons. The army is responding with whatever they have. The dry sounds of shotguns and the louder echoes of grenades fill the air, mixed with the smell of tires and petards thrown by the reds. I stay there for about an hour and a half, watching the sun go down as the intensity of the shooting increases. Behind the line, an old man in dark gear and a helmet, just like most of the people there, directs the movement of the people and the positioning of the tires.

The situation remains stable for a while with people on this side keeping the smoke as thick as possible and the military shooting in this direction. Small explosions fill the air in the middle of Rama IV. From a building constantly chipped by bullets on the opposite side of the road, another group of red shirts (none of them actually wearing red at this point) are communicating with this side about their situation. The man who directs the operation shouts: "Speak in Khmer so they can't understand!" I'm not sure if it is effective with the military but it definitely is with me. As the sun goes down most of the journalists leave. Today is not the right day to be around once night arrives.

I wake up really late this morning, woken up by a loud explosion. Outside the window a thick black smoke cloud fills the sky, darkening my room. I decide to ride down there and take a look, following a tweet that suggested the local petrol station has been set on fire. Outside my house, in the calm that reigns during the day, a woman is selling sweetbread door to door. "The people in some *sois* here cannot exit their homes and many others are scared to go on to the streets to buy food so I decided to go around and sell some food." I greet her and ride to Ngam Duphli. The *soi* is more crowded than yesterday. Walking along the walls on the left side of the *soi* to hide from snipers is more difficult. The front of the *soi* has been closed with a barricade of tires, this time not burning. Without smoke it is possible to see the other side of Rama IV, where a similar group of red shirts is clustered at the beginning of a small *soi*. A family is leaving from a nearby house, with some belongings stuffed into a big green bag, moving for some days to a friend's house in another part of Bangkok. Many people in the area, Thai and foreigners, are doing the same, scared away by the potential expansion of the conflict, as others stock food and beverages in the house, ready to be cut off from the rest of the city. The people hidden behind the barricade occasionally throw a firework in the direction of a building on the other side of Rama IV, where they say snipers have been seen. Every successful firework is met with a cheer and a clap for the launcher. Down Rama IV, the soldiers keep shooting in this direction, but no rubber bullets fall on the street anymore. "They have finished the rubber bullets," one man tells me, as he pulls down his white mask, "now it is just the real ones." We talk for a bit and he tells me that the situation inside Ratchaprasong area is very hard. Early in the morning he found a way in and was told that food is getting scarce and people are very afraid, even if no actual fighting is going on there.

The motorcycle-taxi guy who has been organizing the movement of people there is still shouting directions to everybody from a few meters away. The group at the front is made up of six or seven young Thai in black shirts and an equal number of journalists in blue bulletproof vests and blue reinforced helmets. The number of journalists compared to the protesters gives the scene a funny look, perfectly emblematic of the incestuous relationship between reality and perception through the media. After a while, a *tuk-tuk* stuffed with food and water arrives in the *soi* and drops four big bags of white carton containers filled with rice and plain omelets. I sit there, watching the people taking turns to sit at the front and come back to eat. A young man arrives with about ten big fireworks. I decide then to move down to the Rama IV intersection towards Khlong Toei slum. Here about five hundred people are gathered. They say they are too far away to be reached by the bullets of the army, but they constantly watch the buildings, especially the Siam Commercial Bank down Rama IV, where snipers were shooting the day before. Early in the morning, an old man says, two people were shot here by a yellow shirt from one of the buildings. The area has been totally claimed by the protesters who have built tire barricades on each of the four entrances, exits to the elevated highway, and two lines of barricades extending the whole of Rama IV. Three of those barricades are burning, as people from the side of Rama IV, protected under the highway, roll tires to the people hiding behind the barricade who constantly refurbish the burned ones. At the back, in the direction of Khlong Toei, a line of parked motorcycles divides the "dangerous area" from the "safe one," as people explain to me, but the distinction hardly seems real. Behind this line, a huge crowd of probably a couple of thousand people stretches down the road where a rudimentary stage has been set up a couple of days ago. Motorcycles are parked everywhere, peppered among cars and taxis.

The police booth right under the highway has been claimed as a sort of "war room" in which some of the leaders hold discussions, emerging occasionally to direct the constant delivery of new tires by big pickups and to tell the crowd to take it easy and stay calm. As I talk with some motorcycle-taxi drivers whom I know, a big pickup brings food to the area and a motorcycle-taxi driver uses a traffic cone to direct people into making a queue to get the food, one box and one water bottle each. Another man in black gear comes around and starts calling people to bring their bikes and go with him to an undisclosed place. He wants fifty of them. The call awakens the crowd as people run to take their motorcycles and join the group that is forming underneath the highway. Every new bike is welcomed by the cheering crowd. Some people are shouting not to take pictures at this moment so I put my camera away. People are covering their license plates with opened boxes and the motorcycle-taxi drivers in the crowd take off their vests. One man in the middle of the group tucks a big axe into the pants belted around his bare torso and puts on a military jacket to hide it. The deafening sound of a sniper gun, a scream, and people running away from the corner of Rama IV breaks the moment. An ambulance drives through the crowd hastily and picks up an injured man down Rama IV. When I turn around the small motorcycle detachment is already gone. A few hundred people wait, hidden under the bridge, to see how the situation evolves.

I decide to ride back in the direction of Bon Kai, as the red light of sunset refracts and diffuses into the smoke coming from that direction. On the way, a guard with a headphone in his ear stands in front of a tire shop, maybe patrolling their source. In the whole area, well into the maze of small backstreets where the red shirts are hiding, the air is filled with the scent of burning rubber. Every *soi* that goes out into Rama IV looks the same: a half-crowded narrow street with a thick wall of smoke and fire at the end and constant launches of Molotovs to keep the tires burning. Again the sound of bullets from the military fills Rama IV. Away from Ngam Duphli, however, people move freely in the *sois*, not concerned about snipers. I sit in Soi Sawan Sawat for a while as darkness conquers the area, shapes of men carved into the red flames. I decide to go back to Ngam Duphli and check the situation there. The *soi* now is almost empty and totally dark, no fire, no light. I sit halfway down the *soi* with a group of people on motorcycles who tell me it is too dangerous to go forward.

Today all of these back *sois* are filled with people, discussing or just listening to the evolving events, with many more in the houses looking out. An older woman shows me a photocopy of an unidentifiable picture of dead bodies, claiming they belong to soldiers who refused to shoot and were brought back to their military camps and shot dead. To me it looks like a gray image with a couple of unidentifiable faces. She asks me to take a picture of it and inform the people of the world. I tell her I can barely see anything and I go back to the motorcycle crowd. One of them offers to show me where the snipers are. He gives me a tour of Soi Goethe and explains how to recognize what weapons are being used. Short dry sound: sniper. Longer clear sound: rifle. Dry loud explosion: M79. He imitates the sounds and translates the noises that we hear around. He speaks quietly, hiding in the darkness and moving carefully in the spaces between buildings. A loud explosion fills the air. "This is us," he smiles. "When it is this loud, it is just firecrackers." The soi is interrupted by a low barricade of sandbags, covered with dark green cloth. "To prevent the army from coming here from Sathorn Soi 1," he says, pointing silently to a tall building overlooking the area. "They are there," he whispers, "be very careful." This section of the soi, right before the Goethe Institute, is really dark. I can just feel people wearing black moving around me without really seeing them. I don't like this place so I decide to go back and check again at the Rama IV intersection.

The situation is pretty much the same as before but the crowd is much smaller and the frequency of the shootings has relaxed. The tenth person today comes in my direction and asks me if I think that the UN will intervene and I give my by-now standard answer, explaining the problem for the UN in intervening in internal matters. He looks at me discouraged, lights a cigarette, and stares into the darkness. I leave the area, way too dangerous at this point, and walk in the direction of the stage at Khlong Toei. People sit in front of a small stage made from what looks like a very big table. The speakers, mostly organizers from the nearby slum, step up for a short while, demanding that the government "stop killing the people," interspersed with red-shirt songs, to which some of the listeners dance on the street pavement around the stage. The atmosphere is similar to a village fair, translated into the middle of this gigantic city: street vendors, families hanging around, people sitting on motorcycles, and a constant flow of people walking up and down.

I see a couple of motorcycle-taxi riders whom I know and chat with them, showing my pictures and explaining what I had seen down Rama IV. Every time this happens, a small crowd comes to view the pictures, ask for information, and tell me that in Din Daeng some soldiers are not Thai but Khmer, people brought in by Newin and paid to do a job that fellow Thai refuse. Whether true or not, these rumors, as others flooding the protest, are a fantastic commentary on collective fears, nationalistic sentiments, the red shirts' perception of their enemies, and their personal attempts to make sense of the situation, not wanting to believe that fellow Thai dressed in uniform are indiscriminately shooting at them. Disbelief and hunger for news mix in the streets of Bangkok. I walk to the stage where a local Khlong Toei organizer tells me that they are going to build stages like this all across the city, as they already have done at Victory Monument, reproducing and fragmenting the protest in Ratchaprasong. The atmosphere of a peaceful village fair, however, only takes a minute to change into dense and silencing fear. As I stand behind the stage, the lights go out throughout Rama IV, and a loud explosion tears the joyful mood. Silence descends. People frantically help the speaker down from the stage. Others stand up from the pavement. The minute of dense tension and frantic activity eases when the light returns, and the next speaker comes to the stage.

leave the house hoping to visit the five new stages that the red shirts have put up around the city and talk to the monks who have been chanting at Victory Monument to call for peace. I ride down an empty Sathorn Road dotted by burned phone booths. Towards Lumphini Park the military lines stand in silence, patrolling the emptiness. At the corner with Convent Road, somebody has put an iron statue of two people in black twisted in a fight, another piece of art that will disappear as the area calms down. I ride up Narathiwat Road and turn into Surawong Road, where small crowds of people venture out of their homes to take a look at the situation. My first military checkpoint. I pass through easily with the excuse of visiting a friend's house. Down Surawong, I turn into Rama IV Road, in the direction of MBK department store. Second checkpoint. The street is completely empty, just some soldiers here and there and a column of smoke coming from the Sala Daeng area. The air is heavy, filled with the smoke of burning tires.

I exit the military zone at the corner with Ratchathewi Road, this time after being checked by a soldier, a young man opens his motorcycle seat to reveal a compartment full of ten-baht coins, wrapped in plastic bags. I ride towards Hualamphong Station and then along Rama VI Road until I reach the Aree area. Here the city seems to ignore what is going on a few kilometers away. The usual shoppers and street vendors fill the street with their pungent smell of delicious food. I turn back in the direction of Victory Monument, an hour-long ride for what normally would take twenty minutes, despite the lack of traffic. As I pass the offices of Channel 5 TV station, police officers are setting up a roadblock. At the entrance of the highway right before Victory Monument, the red shirts are replying with their own roadblock. A big crowd of motorcyclists and others are busily piling up plastic barriers and wood in the middle of the street, ready to burn. "The army is coming," shouts a motorcycle-taxi driver as many people move in the direction of Victory Monument. Goodbye peacefulness today.

I ride into a back *soi* to reach Victory Monument but end up in a small closed community where police officers in anti-riot gear lounge inside a compound, taking pictures of what is going on in the street. I ride back and pass the red-shirt barricade to reach Victory Monument. The square is surreal, completely empty with a few groups of curious onlookers standing on the long overpasses. Again, stillness is accentuated by the memories of this buzzing transportation node. A long line of police officers, in uniforms but without weapons or protective gear, crosses the roundabout and stops underneath a tent at the northern side of the square. As they pass, the crowd quietly salutes them. I ask around and a woman tells me that they came to prevent the army attacking from Phahon Yothin Road, surrounding the red shirts. She also tells me that the only way out of the area is towards Ratchawithi Road, as the other two exits are blocked, one by a military line and the other by heavy fighting in what the military declared a "free fire zone," a nice way of saying, "We will shoot everything that moves." Slowly the police officers take up position in rows and move to Phahon Yothin Road where the red shirts' burning barricade is releasing thick black smoke. The police spread out beyond the barricade and start extinguishing the fire. The crowd looks confused, trying to understand their role. From a small gate beside the highway entrance, groups of anti-riot police exit from their refuge and take up position at the right side of the crowd. An old policeman tells protesters to let them do their job and reassures them that they are here to protect the people. Loud applause follows his words.

The police take charge of the situation, rapidly removing the barricade and putting out the fire. The smoke turns white. Never in my life had I thought I would see the police dismantling a just-built barricade being cheered by the same people who put it up. Only smoking debris remains in the middle of the big road as the police take up position again in rows and the anti-riot group goes back to where they came from. An old police officer, who acts as the person in charge, stands in the middle of the street and tells a small crowd of mostly motorcycle-taxi drivers to be calm and that if they don't block the street the military will not arrive. "Do you believe me?" he ends. "Believe" is the common answer as people applaud and cheer the police battalion moving back into Victory Monument and leaving the area.

I decide to take a look in the direction of Ratchaprarop Road, without getting too close. At that side of the roundabout a much bigger crowd is chatting and sitting on at least two hundred motorcycles parked everywhere. I have never seen this many motorcycle-taxi drivers at the protest since the violent turn. I recognize some of them. We exchange information about what is going on in different parts of the city for a short while and then part ways, but only after having wished each other good luck and reminded each other to be careful. Same routine over and over.

I decide to keep going down the street as people in the small alley are collecting big objects to put up more barricades. In the middle of the empty street, crowded only on the sides, a guy sits on his motorbike, in front of a public phone that has been taken out of the booth and left there. I walk past him, smiling at the odd scene, and sit for a while at Soi 6, as smoke from Ratchaprarop hugs a flyover. A small group of people hiding under the flyover are rolling tires into the smoke to be picked up by other hands down the street, I assume. Some people point in the direction of the Century Park Hotel that overlooks the area. They ask me to take pictures in that direction with the zoom. Lucky shot. I zoom with my camera and catch two shapes that look like military guys, kneeling among plants on a high balcony, looking down at the street.

Immediately the news spreads and I am approached by a mass of people asking to see my camera screen. They declare that the balcony is full of snipers, clearly visible. I keep repeating that there are two at most but it takes only an instant for the story to grow bigger. Images in this situation come to play a strangely authoritative role. Even blurry images become a higher form of truth. Nowhere else have I felt this more strongly than in that small *soi* close to a cloud of smoke. The number of people who want to see the images through my camera seems endless. Again, again, again. My camera keeps turning off so I have to zoom again so people can take their own pictures of my camera screen. Pictures of pictures, often taken with a small cell phone camera. Small pixilated images of truth, the first victim in this kind of situation. People here seem, however, bent on not losing it, determined to retain some trace of the truth, stored in their cell phone or memory card. Soon a camera crew arrives and wants to shoot my small camera screen. I show the picture over and over again. I'm no longer sure the shapes are snipers, perhaps only some strange shadows. After a while I decide to walk back to Victory Monument. People are distributing food and water that arrived in a pickup. I see a motorcycle-taxi driver I have met before at the protest site. I tell him that I am surprised to see so many motorcycle-taxi drivers around and he replies that it has been like this in street protests since 1992. "I was there," he says "hiding in a temple when the military shot people in the street. This time is not like that. On that day the soldiers fired straight at people, so many." Funny to have this conversation on May 17, on this bloody anniversary of the events of eighteen years before. I ask for his phone number to interview him on those events. "Call me later on," he says. "Now there is no time and besides that, interviewing now is a very dangerous thing. You may get shot." His sour smile fails to open up his face as he recalls the recent death of Seh Daeng.

I show him the picture I just took and in a second another flow of people begins, taking pictures of my camera screen, asking me to send it to the red-shirt leaders and put the picture on the internet. A guy asks me if I will stay long enough for him to come back with his computer. People are starving for "evidence" or just crumbs of it. I notice, however, that many of them do not really look at the picture to see what it shows but rather to find something they want to see, like the old woman who showed me the photocopy of an indistinguishable picture of alleged bodies of military men killed by other soldiers. A Thai journalist arrives and pulls out a small notebook. I pass him the camera, happy for him to handle the pressure and requests that come with that blurry frame. I decide to ride away. People thank me and offer food and water. I grab a bottle of water and ride back to the Rama IV area. In both the Ngam Duphli and Sawan Sawat areas the situation is stable, military shooting, protesters hidden behind the corners of the *sois* and tire barricades. I stay there for a while watching the tense faces of people who are being shot at close by. They are almost getting used to the sounds of shots and explosions over the last three days, but are still interpreting them for newcomers. "Rifle, rifle, M16, M16, M16, us, us, us, sniper." A large tire barricade has been built across one lane of Rama IV Road, twenty meters east of Sawan Sawat. Behind it, about fifteen men hide in silence, eating grilled pork and sticky rice. Cameras and cell phones are taking videos everywhere. One man, completely covered in black stains from carrying tires, asks me where I am from and tells me he is a supporter of Inter Milan. We are on the same side, I tell him. A younger man on his left tells me he likes Manchester United. Bullets pass over our heads. "Red devils," he laughs as he shows me a UDD scarf wrapped around his waist.

As violence rages in Bangkok's central business district, the conflict enters neighborhoods, homes, and bodies, conquering the senses, one after the other. Close to areas of confrontation, you are hit by a wall of smell from garbage, fermenting in the sun. As electricity and water are cut off by the government, as it tries to ferret out the protesters and hamper their movements, garbage is left unattended in the protest area. Plastic bags full of the remains of the meals that are constantly delivered to the protesters by auto-rickshaws pile up in the streets, mixed with exploded fireworks and glass. Soundscapes have also been altered by the fighting. More and more people listen attentively, trying to decode the army weaponry by its sounds. A sonic knowledge spreads in the area, decoded by people and passed on to a newcomer. Each sound and echo is carefully collected and identified. People keep an ear cocked for the short dry sound of snipers. "Pe, pe, pe." People click their lips to reproduce the sound. Eyes are also on the watch, scanning the area for suspicious movements and the skies for hidden maneuvers on the roofs. Cameras capture images, collecting evidence or just personal memories of this moment. In these situations of danger, senses are the first to be triggered, sharpened to serve their primal purpose of survival.

wake up to the sound of rain trickling on my windows instead of the usual shots. A moment of relief for the people in the street, I think. The illusion does not last long, torn by a loud blast. As soon as the rain stops, I ride towards Ngam Duphli passing an empty Suan Phlu where most of the shops have been closed, especially the ubiquitous 7-Elevens, whose windows are covered with newspapers. The situation in Ngam Duphli is stable now with people hidden behind the tire barricade, few journalists around, and no sound from the military who have moved back to the Lumphini Park area. The atmosphere is much more relaxed. Behind the barricades, people joke for the amusement of journalists. A couple of young men throw fireworks on the street and even venture into the middle of Rama IV Road. A guy in a green and white helmet shouts to the foreign journalists in English: "Do you want to see our snipers? Take your cameras. We will give you our snipers. Take picture." People around laugh loudly. The guy pulls out a small metal tube and uses it to launch a small firework. "Snipers, snipers. Tell the world," the guy repeats. People crack up, squatting at the barricade. "Wait, wait, hey you want to see M79? Here M79." He turns to a very young guy and tells him in Thai to pick something from his bag. He searches frantically in the bag and runs to the middle of Rama IV. Bigger firework, very loud. Again everybody laughs. I walk back to the street. People are discussing the snipers' presence in the zone. I show them my picture from yesterday and they ask me to take some pictures of the roofs above us, to see if the camera catches any snipers. I wait, hidden behind a wall but I see nothing. From the back of the *soi* a man dressed in black pulls a handmade rocket launcher out of his backpack and aims at a tall building above us. One shot explodes in the air. He moves down the wall as everybody squats. "They know we are shooting," someone says. The young man runs up and down the wall looking for a good spot for a second launch. Another loud bang.

I decide to check the situation in Sawan Sawat, and reach Lumphini Tower from a small garden beside the *soi*. At the entrance of the alley the barrier has grown into a barricade of tires. Nobody stands behind it. I go back into the *soi* and enter a small park through an opening in the corrugated iron fence. A man sits close to the entrance. I ask him if it is possible to go this way, and he stands up, completely covered in filth. He is one of the many local homeless who are suddenly finding a social role in this conflict, helping to carry tires, getting free food, or just hanging around. He tells me, "It's impossible for us. We don't have money, we don't have connections." I turn around puzzled. Two friends sit eating at a small table. One of them taps his index fingers on his temple to tell me that the guy is a bit off. What he said, however, seems to make perfect sense to me. I step into the small park where some shacks have been built. On the ground is a mixture of garbage, empty glass bottles, dirty teddy bears. A vicious-looking dog sits on a broken sofa outside a shack. I move in silence and see others walking through the park in the direction of Lumphini Tower. I turn left underneath a long tree branch and pass the first tire barrier outside the soi where I was yesterday. The wall of Lumphini Tower is in front of me. A large iron grating rests on the wall, making an unstable ladder. A man appears at the top of the wall and signals me to go up. This really feels like urban guerrilla warfare.

I walk up the grating and find myself at the entrance to a small building at the side of Lumphini Tower. Three men sit on plastic chairs, lounging and laughing. I sit at the entrance of a small security guardhouse that has been taken over as a relaxing area. They make fun of me for moving carefully. "No danger here," they say calmly. An older man completely covered in black stains takes a splinter out of his plastic flip-flop and prepares a slingshot, holding marbles in his hand. I take some pictures of a devastated Rama IV Road as the men there tell me to go out to the middle of the street. I prefer to live, I tell them. They laugh and say that every time the shooting starts, the *farang* journalists are the first to run away. I decide to keep going toward Lumphini Tower as only the sounds of fireworks fills the air. I walk to the next wall. Ladder going up, another grating going down. A man points out the bullet marks on buildings on the opposite side of Rama IV. "That side is more dangerous than here," he says. I notice a big group of journalists in black vests in a small *soi* at the side of the building. I walk up to the entrance of Lumphini Tower. The monumental patio outside is swarming with relaxed red shirts sitting, eating, smoking, discussing. On the western corner of the patio, behind a thick column, a group of three young Thai sit around two women, one a German journalist and the other a young Thai, asking questions. A period of calm gives a chance to talk to each other.

I sit on a huge flower vase and listen to the conversation, translating from time to time for the German journalist in exchange for using her pen. Sweet deal. The man talks about the problem with this government, their inability to make ends meet, and the lack of fairness in the system and the current situation. The woman responds: "What about the pictures of armed red shirts, of people carrying heavy weapons?" A vocal man, who sets up stages for a living, stands in front of her in an imposing posture. "Where are these pictures? I want to see them. Can you give them to me?" "The website is blocked in Thailand," she replies. "How did you see them then?" "I haven't seen them." "Uhhmmm." The guy turns, looking with a smile at the people around him. "You like yellow shirts?" he pushes. "You watch ASTV, right?" "I know ASTV is partisan and has an agenda. I am interested in listening to both sides, in understanding." "Tell me then why is it that ASTV, which supports the yellow shirts, is open while the red television is closed?" Check. Another man steps up. "We don't have connections," he states, turning around and walking away.

They are grilling her. She came here to ask questions but the tables have been turned. It's refreshing to hear somebody who stands in the middle, believing parts of the government version, discussing with people who a few years ago would never have confronted her in this tone. "I want to hear something," the man says. "Give me one reason why you support the yellow shirts." He raises his voice, "One reason." She interrupts him and says: "Please put on your mask. You are spitting on me." Feeling pressed, I guess, he puts the mask up and then takes it down. "OK. I'll speak normally." He repeats: "Give me one reason why you support the yellow shirts." She stays silent for a second, her dark eyes, framed in large square brown glasses, squeezed tight. "I'm not yellow. My parents are yellow. I just want to understand." "You are yellow," he insists. "Brother,"

I tell him, "if she was 100 percent yellow she would not be here. At least she is trying to see with her eyes." "Yes," she steps forward, "if I were yellow I would do this," and she stands on her toes miming a disgusted face. "You see," he says, finally calm, "if they didn't want to kill people they would throw tear gas and then come here and pick us up, put us in jail, but instead they shoot at us. It would be simple to disperse but they don't." Checkmate. He keeps going. "There is no fairness. This way is going to be a war. Do you think that if Abhisit attacks Ratchaprasong and kills five hundred or a thousand people he could remain?" "No," they both say together. "It would be war," he concludes. A moment of silence. "You see," he adds, "this is democracy. Discussing in this way." A younger man, a motorcycle-taxi driver in the area, calls me and asks me to take a picture of a tall building behind the area with the zoom to see if there are snipers. I walk with him. Nothing on the roof. I show him again the picture from yesterday and he asks for my website so he can copy the photo. I write down the name on a thin cigarette paper, say goodbye, and make my way back to the grating. "Be careful," we echo each other.

Trying to make sense

Today was a day for Thai society to take a breath and look around. I had my second illuminating discussion of the day with a student of Chulalongkorn University. The central question was: How do we make sense of people thinking that red shirts deserve to die at the hands of the army? Interestingly, her first response reflects her class background and upbringing in a struggling family that understands what it means to suffer from inequality. Her friends have been, as she puts it, "raised in good families," so they find it hard to understand what these people are asking for. The question then becomes for her how a "good person," a moderate member of society, comes to think that the state has the right, or rather the duty, to kill people for disrupting life in a commercial area of the city? Or, to put it in the way our friends who side with the military would, how is it that a "peaceful nation under an excellent genius king" comes to be so divided? How did the land of smiles suddenly turn into the land of tense faces?

These questions are running through Thai society these days, on both sides of the red/yellow divide. They are repeatedly discussed among friends, at street corners, on the web. As the student puts it, "People around me are feeling sad and depressed," and these feelings are flowing around, carved on disoriented faces. What happened to us? We talk for a while, trying to make sense of this situation. Thailand has had ten coup d'états since 1971, the highest rate in the world. It has suffered from a long insurgency in the south, washed in the blood of thousands of citizens. Thailand ranks ninth in the world for the number of murders per year and fourteenth for murders per capita. Thai murderers like guns. Thailand ranks first in the world for the percentage of homicides committed by firearms. The idea of the peaceful unified nation, evidently more a way in which Thai society thinks of itself rather than a social reality, lies at the roots of the modern Thai state, organized around the triad of "Nation, Buddhism, and King," proposed by King Rama VI and repeated over and over again in every school of the kingdom. For a century, the concept has been propagated through many effective techniques, from textbooks to nationwide campaigns, from tourist slogans to TV advertisements. The MoSo campaign, launched by the government with the support of the Internal Security Operations Command (another book should be written on ISOC, from its anti-communist origins to its present role), is a good example of these techniques: the latest chapter in a centuries-long attempt by the Thai state to transform desirable, but not always prevalent, individual behavior into national character. As always, hegemonic projects remain incomplete. Despite constant efforts to fill in the cracks that emerge along the way, the project finally stumbles into them, leaving people puzzled and suddenly facing a ravine.

"What position do we take if one says that it is an old system that we are living under. It's rotten, but nothing can be changed. It's one of the questions my best friend asks me," she adds. The conversation gets philosophical. It is the old Hamlet question: is it better to accept a known reality, with all its pitfalls, or to jump on to a new stage, taking a step into the dark? Humanity divides over this question and Thai society is no exception. "Yes" she replies to herself, "there are people who don't believe they can change or have the power. We must create the system not just let the system control us. Many NGOs work for the grassroots but they don't believe in the people." Silence for a second. I say, "I think many people believe things can change but just don't want them to. I think if we look at the yellow shirts as people who don't believe they can change stuff, we are making things too simple, assuming that deep inside they think things do need to be changed. Many people want things to be the same and not only for personal benefit, maybe also for that very human fear of the dark." "I see your point, but that seems to be very passive," she says, discouraged. "Or very active in preserving things," I intervene. "Some of them have been anything but passive. They actively took a position, went to Silom to protest, pressed the government, put themselves at risk at Victory Monument. They actively want things to remain as they are." She pauses. "So some people want to be ruled and some people don't," she concludes, dissatisfied.

INSIGHTFUL, IN TREND, INDEPENDENT

THE NATION

FUJI xerox

THAILAND · THURSDAY, May 20, 2010 / 32 PAGES / 3 SECTIONS / VOLUME 35, NO 52603 / Bt30

FIERY ANARCHY

THAILAND'S BLACKEST DAY

>> CURFEW FROM 8PM TO 6AM
>> **TROOPS STORM LUMPINI**
>> RED LEADERS END RALLY AND SURRENDER
>> **PROTESTERS RUN AMOK**
>> CENTRALWORLD BURNS

>> **HECTIC EVACUATIONS IN MANY AREAS**
>> REDS ON RAMPAGE IN UDON, KHON KAEN AND SEVERAL OTHER PROVINCES
>> MOBS TARGET REPORTERS

>> SIAM THEATRE GUTTED, COLLAPSES
>> **CHANNEL 3 ATTACKED, OFF AIR**
>> NEWS OUTLETS CUT DOWN SERVICES, SUSPEND EDITIONS
>> ARSONISTS SHOOT AT FIREMEN

After six days of heavy fighting around the original protest area, the military this morning launched the final dispersal of the red shirts. I turn on the TV and see tanks moving onto the barricades and pushing them down. The face of the government spokesman, Panitan Wattanayakorn, appears on every channel, assuring the population that this is being done for their own safety and that the situation is under control. I look out of the window. A big smoke column coils into the sky in the direction of Rama IV Road. The situation hardly seems under control. It is not the usual black smoke from tires but a bigger gray cloud. I wait for the sound of shots to slacken then ride my bike to Ngam Duphli. The street has just been destroyed. Buildings along Rama IV are burning: bank branches, convenience stores, and some ATM machines. A few people I have never seen before are walking around, taking pictures and helping to put out small fires. The street is covered in filth, food everywhere fermenting in the hot sun. A small crowd hidden behind a wall stares at a tall building overlooking the *soi*, trying to spot snipers. The entrance to the *soi* is completely open, no tires left. The building at the corner of Rama IV Road, an office of Kasikorn Bank, has been completely burned, leaving an empty blackened shell with electric wires swinging from the pole on the street. The building is dripping with water used to put out the fire. In front of this burned skeleton of a building sit two men, one a local resident, the other a Thai journalist. They casually discuss what is going on around the city, in a mixture of excitement and disbelief. I talk to them for a while and then walk with the Thai journalist down to Rama IV. Turning out of Ngam Duphli, we pass a barricade of tires stretching across Rama IV Road, and walk into a destroyed area, burned buildings and phone booths, smashed ATMs, and a thick layer of burned rubber everywhere. The pavement is sticky, the air is dense. People are taking pictures, walking in stunned silence. Bank branches and 7-Elevens have been burned with surgical precision, somehow managing to keep the adjacent buildings undamaged.

The street is completely covered in debris. I keep walking down the big road. A man who is taking pictures stops and stares at a burned phone booth thrown on the ground. Somehow he does not seem to be able to stand this sight, though he was happily photographing the burned buildings. He stands there, silent. I stand close to him. "How do you feel about what is going on?" I ask. "Very bad," he says without taking his eyes off the phone booth. "Very, very bad. And now the leaders have fled, it is free. Everybody can do whatever they want." He moves to stare at the street, the tension accumulating on his forehead. He stares at me and suddenly snaps out, "Where are you from?" "Italy" I reply distractedly. "I am sorry, an Italian journalist just died." "I am sorry too, for many Thai." I walk away, leaving him standing there, stamped on his face the same worries you see on people from both sides of the political spectrum, on friends as they sip a beer, on passersby as they go about their daily business. I keep walking with the Thai journalist. We pass in front of Lumphini Tower, where great political conversations were held yesterday and where now there is only emptiness and trash. The small guardhouse where people were lounging yesterday starts burning in front of us. Three guys run up with fire extinguishers, trying in vain to put out the fire. One of them stops to pick up his phone; another guy from nearby Soi Sawan Sawat picks up the fire extinguisher and takes over his job. "Lower, lower!" a man shouts. I squat automatically, scared that someone is shooting. A huge splash of water comes from a nearby garden, through the burning house. I feel really stupid. I enter the garden through an opening in the corrugated iron. Four men come out of Soi Sawan Sawat with a fire hose. Soon the gray smoke turns white as the fire goes out. I walk through the park to the *soi*, where another small crowd stands, looking disoriented. For the first time in days I see women in the Bon Kai area. I walk towards the highway bridge on Rama IV. "This section is really empty," the Thai journalist says. "It scares me."

We walk in the direction of Khlong Toei, attracted by a huge smoke cloud, the one I saw from my home. A power plant is on fire, cutting electricity all the way to Sathorn. The flames have extended to a nearby building. Two fire trucks stand in front of the building, not wasting water trying to put it out. Underneath the highway bridge, people take pictures and a crowd of about fifteen police officers chat with locals. On both of the columns that support the bridge a large white cloth poses a haunting question in red paint: "Father, where are you?"

I stay there for a while watching the smoke slowly embrace the building, occasionally revealing the high flames behind. The small police booth that was used as a "war room" is also on fire. I walk to a motorcycle-taxi driver and ask what is going on in other areas. "The protest has been cleared. Buildings are being set on fire around the city: Central World, Siam Paragon, Siam Center." "Really?" I ask, dumbstruck. "I'm sorry," he apologizes to me for a reason I do not understand. I ask him to drive me back to Ngam Duphli to grab my bike. As he drives through the back *sois* infested with garbage left uncollected for almost a week, a small plane passes over our heads with a loudspeaker broadcasting something I cannot understand. He drops me by my bike. An old woman walks past us. She looks like the people one normally meets when walking these *sois*, local dwellers or street vendors, standing on sidewalks selling food or drinks. She is in her fifties, dark skinned, thin hair turning gray. She is wearing a white apron with small red flowers. The small plane passes again. A woman's voice says through the loudspeakers, "The leaders of the protest have already surrendered. The military are retreating. Please stop." I ask the old woman, "Do you think the people will accept this?" "They will," she says. "It is finished." She does not look comforted or relieved. I walk to the beginning of the *soi*. A man with a big fire hose is putting out a small fire and throwing water on the tire barricade on Rama IV to prevent it from burning. He then stands in the middle of the street, pouring water on himself. Others call out to him by name and direct him to another small fire inside the Kasikorn Bank building. I ask a motorcycle-taxi driver if he thinks the people will accept what the plane lady said and go home. "We live here," he says. "We are people of this area who came out to see and to look after the place. The fighters went away into Khlong Toei hours ago." What will they do now, or as a Thai friend put it tonight, "How can I sustain my lifestyle now? How can we restore this country?"

These questions will keep people in Bangkok awake tonight, stuck inside their homes by the government's curfew.

I go out again in the late afternoon, trying to get to the Ratchaprasong area before the sun goes down and the curfew kicks in. I ride towards Silom and walk to the first military roadblock in Convent Road. The Thai passing through are registered by a soldier sitting at a small table on the side of the street. I ask the two soldiers at the roadblock if it is true that both Central World and Siam Paragon are burning. The young officer looks at me confused with deep dark eyes. I ask again. "I don't know where these places are," he answers. "I don't know Bangkok." Great way to keep your soldier safe during a conflict in an urban setting. I walk to a completely empty and very dark Silom Road. Three armored vehicles are parked in the middle of the street on the opposite side. Some soldiers sit around them with their uniforms hanging half open, laughing. A line of soldiers walks down from Ratchadamri with very tired faces. I smile at them, but they don't smile back. The Sala Daeng intersection is completely different from the last time I was there. The tires and bamboo sticks that used to be a barricade sit in huge piles on the side, close to the statue of King Rama IV. Three bulldozers are lifting up the remains and letting them fall into dark green trucks. Caterpillar tracks are etched into a thin layer of burned rubber on the asphalt. I sit there for a while watching mechanical force removing the weak defenses. A bunch of men in Bangkok Muncipality workers' vests direct the movement with their hands, amid the noise of engines. Unable to talk to them, I wonder how many of them are red-shirt supporters, not only defeated but also already busy clearing the area. I walk down Ratchadamri Road.

The place feels haunted. For the first time since I came to Thailand, I can hear the twitter of birds in an area that is normally smothered by the noise of traffic and, for the last month, by the broadcast speeches. It feels as if the inhabitants have suddenly disappeared, leaving everything behind. Clothes, fans, TV sets, motorcycles, unfinished food, half-cooked rice, piles of vegetables, half-opened tents, monks' clothes, wallets, documents, bags, red paraphernalia, medicines, sealed water bottles still cold. Everything the same as a crowded scene, just with the people erased. The deafening sound of birds echoes in the emptiness. I walk through Ratchadamri, passing a burned-out toilet bus across the street beyond Chulalongkorn Hospital. On the other side of the street a giant pile of black bags of garbage attracts swarms of flies and an incredible number of gray pigeons, picking at leftover food. A few human pigeons do the same, picking timidly through things left behind by the protest, putting the best items in their bags. A man wearing a Bangkok Municipality vest notices I am staring at him as he puts an electric plug into his black and white bag. "Recycle," he tells me, breaking the silence. Further down, three men are piling all the electric appliances they can find on the back of a pickup. The most common item is a fan. I don't think I have ever seen a truck full of fans before.

As I pass Sarasin Road, a group of soldiers sits on the left side of the street. I greet them and they say I cannot go further as the area is not yet secured and there are still snipers around. Four of them sit on the sidewalk. Behind them, in a small space between two buildings, about twenty protesters sit on the ground, their hands tied by a black plastic cord. One guy raises his hands to another's mouth to let him smoke a cigarette he is holding. As I move to take a picture, a soldier picks up a bullet near my feet, hiding it in his pocket. I look around and find another one, take a picture, and then pick it up. I go back to the soldier and ask, "Is this an M16?" He looks at me without saying a word, takes the bullet, turns around, and hides it in his pocket. "Can I have that as a souvenir?" I ask ironically. "How about this as a souvenir?" he asks, showing me the plastic cord used to bind prisoners. I get the message and walk back. A military officer in plain clothes shouts at a young guy walking down Sarasin, "Come here or I shoot." The soldier is holding a phone attached to his belt. "I'll shoot." The guy keeps walking. Another soldier in uniform appears. The guy starts running into a *soi*. I walk back to the entrance of Lumphini Park. There, police officers are taking pictures with their cell phones of red-shirt posters and graffiti left on the wall. A young policeman picks up a red shirt with a picture of Thaksin doing the

Carabao hand sign. He smiles at me and walks away with the shirt. Two other policemen are collecting red paraphernalia. They see my camera and ask me to take a picture of them holding a red-shirt bandana with the words, "Truth Today." They tell me, "We are completely red shirts. The police officers are red shirts. Please report the real news. Please help us." They walk away with the bandana, rescuing "insignificant" pieces of history left behind by the reds.

I walk back to my bike in Silom and try to get into Ratchaprasong that way. The street is completely empty, except for lines of soldiers, protected by razor wire. I pass through the first two lines, just staring straight ahead, ignoring the soldiers. At the third one I get stopped. A handsome old man tells me about the curfew, adding that he cannot be sure it will be safe there after six. I tell him I will just take some pictures and then leave. "Be careful," he says, "they like to shoot journalists." The irony of these words from a soldier is too dry to pass unnoticed. "That is why I do not have a journalist pass," I discover myself saying. "Smart," he replies in this epic of absurdity. I walk down past Chulalongkorn University, hearing shots coming from Ratchaprasong, as the sky turns red and the soldiers seal off the area.

After a long night whose events will remain one of the big question marks of this protest, I wake up and decide to take a look at Ratchaprasong and gauge the extent of the damage left by a day that will raise a host of questions over the role of the military, the police, and the black shirts, the actual number of deaths, and what happened at Wat Pathum Wanaram, a large temple between Central World and Siam Paragon. In the late morning of the nineteenth this temple, assigned as a safe zone for kids and older people leaving the protest, became a stage for underground operations, a meeting place for a small group of armed black shirts, and a killing field for at least six people, allegedly shot dead by soldiers hidden on the Skytrain tracks above. I arrive from Henry Dunant and walk to Rama I with two friends, a Thai guy and a French woman. Along the huge empty street many drains are overflowing with water, creating puddles on the sidewalks and spreading on the street.

Right before the last red-shirt barricade that still blocks the entrance to Rama I Road, a line of metropolitan buses is waiting for people who took refuge in two safe zones and are now in the police headquarters waiting to make their way back home. At the side entrance of the headquarters a big group of people sit on the ground with lost faces, directed by female officers of the border police. A tall monk is standing close to them, staring past the officers talking into a loud speaker in front of him, into the emptiness. Scared eyes look at me, many of them filled with tears, as the police tell them that everything is okay and that they will soon be sent to the train station or to Mo Chit bus terminal. We decide to keep walking.

We pass through a small military checkpoint and walk to the side of Siam Paragon. The atmosphere is completely surreal. Contrary to what I had heard, Siam Paragon is intact, but the building in front has been completely gutted, water dripping everywhere. A few soldiers sit on a handrail, their weapons on their shoulders. The normally shady area underneath the Skytrain seems completely dark. The underbelly of the Skytrain track is pitch black. Dirty water overflows everywhere, swamping everything left behind by the protesters who sought refuge in Wat Pathum and in the police headquarters opposite. In this deathly silence, a loud rhythmic sound fills the air: the continuous and enervating buzz of the alarm of Siam Paragon, accentuating the already post-disaster feeling. Military, police, and a few journalists walk around with wide-open eyes. I go towards the temple. A small box, full of slingshots and Molotov cocktails in small Red Bull bottles, lies in the middle of the street, too visible not to have been placed for journalists to see. The smell of fire fills the air. The sound of the alarm slowly fades. We walk into the front area of the temple, where some objects are left, mostly helmets and clothes. Police share the space with monks and a few onlookers. The rear section of the temple ground is covered with mats. A group of policemen in full riot gear sit in the shade. It is the first time since the beginning of the street protest that I see a tear gas launcher, and in the hands of the police. I chat with two men sitting apart from the group. "It must be hot in that uniform." "Yes, It's very hot and very heavy." They both want to talk, maybe even need to get things out of their system. They say they are on the side of the people and have themselves been under fire from the military. "We have to hide as well," one says. "We are sent here with no weapons and we risk being shot by the army. Yesterday I saw a sniper aiming at me. We couldn't do anything else than hide." He speaks nervously, showing all his frustration of having to be here to clean up the mess that somebody else created. I say goodbye and walk away, ready to see Central World.

On the side of the temple the Zen section of the shopping mall towers over us. The scene is stunning. The building has been completely burned. The orange sign for Zen World has been darkened by the flames and now reads "Zen Word", the burned letter L lying on the ground. The interior is completely devastated. The huge windows at the front have been destroyed. The ground is strewn with broken glass everywhere. Only a little remains of the plastic banner that used to hang down the side of the building. "WOW" it says, before turning into a melted gray mass of plastic. Above that an untouched banner says "Peace." Chance plays strange tricks. This side looks as if a huge black eraser has been rubbed over the shopping center. In front of the building a pool of water reflects the destruction. I am sure around me there are noises, but somehow in my memory the silence is absolute. We keep walking around the building to the front of a protest stage, left there completely empty, mats still on the street pavement. The scene is apocalyptic. The middle section of Central World is just gone, as if a giant spoon had scooped away this delight of Bangkok's landscape. It is breathtaking. It defeats language.

I keep taking pictures, completely oblivious to what is going on around me. My Thai friend snaps me out of it. "They say it is dangerous to be here. The army is coming back. We need to go." I turn around. A police officer is delivering this message from a moving truck. We pass rapidly through the destruction, in deep silence. My Thai friend looks shaken. He keeps muttering, "Fuck. Fuck. Fuck." Over and over again.

MAPS

1 Siam Cinema: Burned to the ground after the dispersal on May 19
2 Silom Road: Grenade attack on April 22
3 Wat Pathum: Designated as a "safe area," but came under attack on May 19
4 Suan Phlu: Area of conflict between May 14 and May 18
5 Chulalongkorn Hospital: Raided various times by the red shirts looking for snipers
6 Sala Daeng intersection: Seh Daeng was shot here on May 13/ Dusit Hotel was attacked
   by RPG during the night of May 17
7 Central World: Set on fire after the dispersal on May 19
8 Ratchaprasong intersection: UDD stage
9 Big C: Attempted arson on May 19
10 Lumphini Park: Area of heavy fighting from May 14
11 Sarasin intersection: Area of heavy fighting from May 13
12 Bon Kai: Area of fighting from May 14/ Arson attacks on May 19 to banks and 7-Eleven
   shops
13 Khlong Toei: Red shirts' gathering area from May 15

RATCHAPRASONG MAP

VICTORY MONUMENT MAP

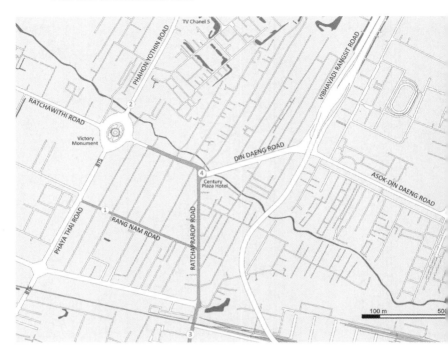

1   Rang Nam Road: Heavy fighting between May 15 and May 18
2   Victory Monument: Light exchanges of fire in the evenings after May 14
3   Ratchaprarop: Declared by the army a "Live Fire Area" on May 15
4   Century Plaza Hotel: Snipers spotted on May 17

PHAN FA BRIDGE MAP

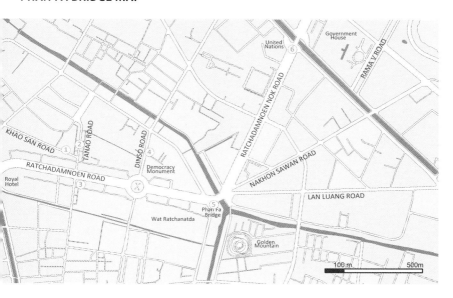

1   Khao San Road: Shrines for the dead protesters
2   Tanao Road: Military attack on foot on April 10
3   14 October, 1973 Memorial
4   Dinso Road: Military attack on April 10/Abandoned tanks
5   Phan Fa Bridge: UDD stage
6   Makkasan Bridge: Early clashes between red shirts and military on April 10

RED JOURNEYS